We hope this book has been informative and helpful on your journey to understanding and celebrating older adults. Thank you for your interest and support!

Title: Global Challenges: Climate Change, Rising Powers, and the Future
Subtitle: Examining Global Challenges, Climate Crisis, Emerging Powers, and Prospects for the Future

Series: Global Perspectives: Exploring World Politics
By Jonathan A. Sinclair

Table of Contents

Introduction **6**

The Interplay of Politics and Global Challenges 6

Significance of Climate Change, Rising Powers, and Future Trends 9

Importance of International Cooperation and Global Governance 14

Chapter 1: Climate Change and Environmental Politics **19**

Understanding Climate Change and its Impacts 19

International Climate Agreements and Commitments...23

Climate Policies and Strategies 28

Climate Change and Security Nexus 33

Chapter 2: Energy Policy and Transition **38**

Global Energy Landscape and Challenges 38

Renewable Energy and Sustainable Development 42

Fossil Fuel Dependency and Transition Strategies 47

Role of International Cooperation in Energy Policy 52

Chapter 3: Rising Powers: India **58**

India's Growing Influence in Global Politics 58

Political System and Democratic Governance 63

Economic Development and Challenges 67

India's Role in Regional and International Relations 71

Chapter 4: Rising Powers: Brazil **76**

Political Landscape and Democratic Institutions 76

Economic Growth and Socioeconomic Inequality 80

Environmental Concerns and Rainforest Preservation .85

Brazil's Engagement in Global Affairs 90

Chapter 5: Rising Powers: Turkey........................**94**

Political System and Governance Challenges 94

Geopolitical Importance and Regional Dynamics..........99

Identity Politics and Social Changes............................ 103

Turkey's Role in Middle Eastern Affairs and Beyond... 107

Chapter 6: Emerging Trends and Future Scenarios

.... **111**

Technological Advancements and Disruptive Innovations

.... 111

Shifting Global Order and Power Redistribution 116

Migration and Refugee Crisis 120

Social Movements and Activism in the 21st Century 125

Chapter 7: Global Stability and Cooperation **130**

The Role of International Organizations in Maintaining

Stability 130

Diplomacy and Conflict Resolution 135

Building Trust and Fostering Dialogue.......................... 139

Promoting Sustainable Development Goals................... 144

Conclusion **149**

Recap of Key Insights on Global Challenges 149

Call to Action for a Sustainable and Cooperative Future

.... 154

The Role of Individuals, Governments, and International

Community 160

Key Terms and Definitions **165**

Supporting Materials..........................**168**

Introduction
The Interplay of Politics and Global Challenges

The world today is confronted with a multitude of complex challenges that transcend borders and require global cooperation. Climate change, rising powers, and future trends have emerged as crucial areas where politics and global challenges intersect. In this introductory chapter, we will explore the interplay between politics and these pressing global issues, highlighting their significance and emphasizing the importance of international cooperation and global governance.

1. Significance of Climate Change, Rising Powers, and Future Trends

1.1 The Urgency of Climate Change

- Understanding the magnitude of climate change and its impacts on ecosystems, economies, and societies.

- Recognizing the need for urgent action to mitigate greenhouse gas emissions, adapt to changing climates, and build resilience.

1.2 The Rise of Emerging Powers

- Shifting global power dynamics and the ascent of emerging powers like India, Brazil, and Turkey.

- Examining the political, economic, and regional influences of these rising powers and their implications for global governance.

1.3 Future Trends and their Implications

- Analyzing emerging trends in technology, demographics, and geopolitics and their potential impact on global stability.

- Considering the challenges and opportunities posed by disruptive innovations, changing power structures, and socio-political movements.

2. Importance of International Cooperation and Global Governance

2.1 The Need for Collective Action

- Understanding that addressing global challenges requires collaborative efforts from all nations.

- Highlighting the interdependence of nations in achieving sustainable development and a secure future.

2.2 International Institutions and Agreements

- Assessing the role of international organizations, such as the United Nations, in fostering cooperation and addressing global challenges.

- Examining key international agreements, including the Paris Agreement and the Sustainable Development Goals, and their effectiveness in driving global action.

2.3 Political Will and Leadership

- Emphasizing the role of political leaders in championing global cooperation and prioritizing sustainable policies.

- Showcasing successful examples of international collaboration and the positive outcomes they have achieved.

2.4 Overcoming Political Barriers

- Recognizing that political interests, divergent priorities, and geopolitical tensions can hinder effective global governance.

- Discussing strategies to bridge political divides, promote dialogue, and foster consensus on critical global challenges.

Conclusion

In this introductory chapter, we have explored the interplay between politics and global challenges. Climate change, rising powers, and future trends have been identified as significant areas requiring immediate attention and international cooperation. We have underscored the importance of collective action, the role of international institutions, and the need for political will and leadership in addressing these challenges.

As we delve deeper into the subsequent chapters, we will examine specific aspects such as climate change and environmental politics, energy policy and transition, and the political systems and dynamics of emerging powers. By analyzing these topics, we aim to gain a comprehensive understanding of the complex web of politics and global challenges and pave the way for a sustainable and cooperative future.

Significance of Climate Change, Rising Powers, and Future Trends

In this chapter, we will delve into the significance of climate change, rising powers, and future trends in the context of global challenges. These interconnected issues shape the trajectory of world politics and have far-reaching implications for the future of our planet and humanity as a whole. Understanding their significance is crucial for addressing the pressing challenges we face today.

1. The Urgency of Climate Change

1.1 Understanding the Magnitude of Climate Change Climate change has emerged as one of the most pressing global challenges of our time. We will explore the scientific evidence behind climate change, including rising global temperatures, melting ice caps, and extreme weather events. By examining these factors, we can grasp the urgency of the situation and its implications for ecosystems, economies, and societies.

1.2 Impacts on Ecosystems and Biodiversity Climate change has profound effects on natural ecosystems and biodiversity. We will discuss the consequences of habitat loss, species extinction, and disruption of ecological balances. Additionally, we will explore the link between climate change and environmental degradation, such as deforestation, pollution, and the depletion of natural resources.

1.3 Socioeconomic Implications Climate change poses significant socioeconomic challenges. We will examine its impact on agriculture, water resources, and public health. The discussion will encompass food security, water scarcity, and the increased vulnerability of marginalized communities to climate-related disasters. Understanding these implications is crucial for devising effective strategies to address the socioeconomic consequences of climate change.

2. The Rise of Emerging Powers

2.1 Shifting Global Power Dynamics The global balance of power is evolving, with emerging powers such as India, Brazil, and Turkey playing increasingly influential roles. We will explore the reasons behind their rise, including economic growth, demographic shifts, and advancements in technology. By analyzing these factors, we can comprehend the changing dynamics of global politics and their implications for global challenges.

2.2 Political, Economic, and Regional Influences Each rising power brings its unique set of political, economic, and regional influences to the global stage. We will delve into the political systems and governance structures of India, Brazil, and Turkey, examining the challenges and opportunities they face. Furthermore, we will explore their economic development trajectories, social inequalities, and regional engagement, shedding light on their role in shaping global challenges.

2.3 Cooperation and Competition The rise of these emerging powers presents both opportunities for cooperation and challenges in terms of competition. We will analyze the cooperation dynamics between these powers and other global actors, such as established powers and international institutions. Additionally, we will explore potential areas of competition, including access to resources, geopolitical rivalries, and conflicting interests.

3. Future Trends and their Implications

3.1 Technological Advancements and Disruptive Innovations The rapid pace of technological advancements brings both promise and uncertainty. We will examine emerging technologies, such as artificial intelligence, renewable energy, and biotechnology, and their potential to address global challenges. Simultaneously, we will analyze the ethical, social, and economic implications of these innovations, including concerns related to privacy, job displacement, and inequality.

3.2 Shifting Global Order and Power Redistribution The global order is undergoing transformation, driven by changing power dynamics and geopolitical shifts. We will explore the implications of these changes for global governance, international cooperation, and the resolution of global challenges. Additionally, we will assess the potential impacts on established institutions and the need for adaptive mechanisms to address emerging global issues.

3.3 Societal Movements and Activism in the 21st Century Social movements and activism have gained prominence in addressing global challenges. We will examine the role of grassroots movements, youth activism, and civil society organizations in driving change. By exploring examples of successful mobilization, we will highlight the transformative power of collective action and its potential to shape the future trajectory of global challenges.

Conclusion

In this chapter, we have delved into the significance of climate change, rising powers, and future trends. We have explored the urgency of addressing climate change, considering its impacts on ecosystems, biodiversity, and socioeconomic systems. Additionally, we have analyzed the rise of emerging powers and their influence on global challenges, emphasizing both the opportunities for cooperation and the potential areas of competition. Lastly, we have examined future trends, including technological advancements and sociopolitical movements, and their implications for addressing global challenges.

By understanding the significance of these issues, we can better grasp the complex interplay between politics and global challenges. This understanding lays the foundation for the subsequent chapters, where we will explore specific aspects such as climate change and environmental politics, energy policy and transition, and the political systems and dynamics of emerging powers.

Importance of International Cooperation and Global Governance

In this chapter, we will explore the critical importance of international cooperation and global governance in addressing global challenges. As the world becomes increasingly interconnected, the need for collaborative efforts and effective governance mechanisms becomes paramount. We will delve into the significance of international cooperation, examine the role of global governance institutions, and discuss the challenges and opportunities in promoting collective action.

1. The Need for Collective Action

1.1 Understanding Interdependence Global challenges, such as climate change, transcend national boundaries and require collective action. We will analyze the interconnected nature of these challenges and the recognition that no single country can tackle them alone. The concept of interdependence underscores the importance of cooperation and shared responsibility in finding solutions.

1.2 Overcoming Global Challenges We will examine specific global challenges, such as climate change, energy security, and poverty eradication, to understand their magnitude and complexity. Through case studies and examples, we will highlight how international cooperation and coordinated efforts are essential for mitigating the impacts of these challenges and achieving sustainable development.

1.3 Multidimensional Benefits International cooperation yields numerous benefits beyond addressing specific challenges. We will discuss the positive externalities of collaboration, including enhanced diplomatic relations, knowledge sharing, and capacity building. Cooperation also fosters innovation, trade, and economic growth, creating a mutually reinforcing cycle of development.

2. International Institutions and Agreements

2.1 Role of International Organizations We will explore the role of international organizations in facilitating global cooperation and governance. Institutions such as the United Nations, World Bank, and World Trade Organization play a crucial role in setting global agendas, coordinating responses, and promoting cooperation among member states. We will examine their mandates, functions, and challenges.

2.2 Global Agreements and Commitments International agreements serve as essential frameworks for global cooperation. We will analyze key agreements, such as the Paris Agreement on climate change and the Sustainable Development Goals, and assess their effectiveness in driving collective action. Furthermore, we will discuss the challenges of implementation and the need for increased accountability.

2.3 Regional and Bilateral Cooperation Cooperation at regional and bilateral levels also plays a vital role in addressing global challenges. We will explore examples of regional organizations, such as the European Union and

African Union, and discuss how regional integration can foster collective action. Additionally, we will examine the significance of bilateral partnerships and collaborations in addressing specific challenges.

3. Political Will and Leadership

3.1 The Role of Political Leaders Effective international cooperation requires political will and leadership. We will analyze the role of political leaders in setting priorities, advocating for cooperation, and mobilizing resources. Through case studies, we will highlight instances of successful leadership and examine the qualities and strategies that contribute to effective global governance.

3.2 Overcoming Political Barriers Political barriers can hinder international cooperation. We will discuss factors such as divergent national interests, power imbalances, and geopolitical tensions that pose challenges to collective action. Strategies for overcoming these barriers, including diplomatic negotiations, consensus-building, and mediation, will be examined.

3.3 Public Engagement and Civil Society The engagement of civil society and public participation are crucial for effective global governance. We will explore the role of non-governmental organizations, grassroots movements, and citizen-led initiatives in influencing global agendas and holding governments accountable. Emphasizing the importance of inclusivity and transparency, we will highlight the potential for bottom-up approaches to drive change.

4. Promoting Global Cooperation

4.1 Science, Technology, and Innovation We will discuss the role of science, technology, and innovation in fostering global cooperation. Through advancements in research, data-sharing, and technological solutions, we can enhance collective understanding of global challenges and develop collaborative strategies for addressing them.

4.2 Education and Awareness Education and awareness play a crucial role in promoting global cooperation. We will explore the significance of education in nurturing global citizenship, fostering empathy, and promoting cross-cultural understanding. Additionally, we will discuss the role of media, communication platforms, and public campaigns in raising awareness about global challenges and the importance of collective action.

4.3 Strengthening Global Governance Mechanisms To enhance international cooperation, we need to strengthen global governance mechanisms. We will discuss potential reforms to international institutions, such as improving representation, accountability, and decision-making processes. Furthermore, we will examine innovative governance models and collaborative platforms that enable participation from diverse stakeholders.

Conclusion

In this chapter, we have emphasized the importance of international cooperation and global governance in addressing global challenges. By recognizing the need for collective action, understanding the role of international institutions and agreements, and acknowledging the significance of political will and leadership, we can foster effective global governance. Furthermore, by promoting public engagement, leveraging science and technology, and strengthening global governance mechanisms, we can pave the way for enhanced cooperation and a more sustainable and equitable future.

Chapter 1: Climate Change and Environmental Politics

Understanding Climate Change and its Impacts

Chapter 1 explores the intricate relationship between climate change and environmental politics. In this section, we will delve into the fundamental aspects of climate change, including its causes, mechanisms, and scientific consensus. By understanding the scientific foundation, we can grasp the magnitude of climate change and its profound impacts on ecosystems, societies, and economies.

1. The Science of Climate Change

1.1 The Greenhouse Effect and the Role of Greenhouse Gases We will explain the greenhouse effect, whereby certain gases in the atmosphere trap heat and regulate Earth's temperature. Understanding the role of greenhouse gases, such as carbon dioxide (CO_2) and methane (CH_4), in intensifying this effect will form the basis for comprehending climate change dynamics.

1.2 Causes of Climate Change We will explore the primary drivers of climate change, including natural factors such as volcanic activity and solar radiation, as well as anthropogenic factors, primarily human activities. The significant contributors, such as fossil fuel combustion, deforestation, and industrial processes, will be discussed in detail, highlighting their influence on the Earth's climate system.

1.3 Scientific Consensus and Climate Models We will examine the overwhelming scientific consensus on climate change, established through rigorous research, data analysis, and peer-reviewed studies. Additionally, we will explore the role of climate models in simulating climate scenarios and predicting future changes, thereby informing policy decisions and adaptation strategies.

2. Impacts on Ecosystems

2.1 Biodiversity Loss and Habitat Disruption Climate change has severe implications for ecosystems and biodiversity. We will discuss the consequences of altered habitats, disrupted migration patterns, and species extinction. Case studies from various ecosystems, such as coral reefs, forests, and polar regions, will illustrate the ecological impacts of climate change.

2.2 Shifts in Ecosystem Services and Resource Availability Climate change affects essential ecosystem services, including water supply, pollination, and soil fertility. We will explore the consequences of disrupted ecosystem functions and their implications for food security, freshwater availability, and the sustainability of natural resources.

2.3 Ocean Acidification and Sea Level Rise Climate change significantly impacts the world's oceans. We will examine the phenomenon of ocean acidification, caused by the absorption of excess CO_2, and its consequences for marine ecosystems and biodiversity. Furthermore, we will discuss sea-level rise and the associated risks to coastal communities, infrastructure, and ecosystems.

3. Socioeconomic Implications

3.1 Food Security and Agriculture Climate change poses risks to global food security and agricultural productivity. We will analyze the impacts of changing weather patterns, extreme weather events, and shifts in growing seasons on crop yields, livestock production, and food distribution. The discussion will encompass strategies for building resilience and adapting agricultural practices.

3.2 Water Resources and Availability Climate change exacerbates water scarcity and affects the availability of freshwater resources. We will examine the impacts on water supply, including changes in precipitation patterns, glacial melt, and the intensification of droughts and floods. Additionally, we will discuss the challenges and solutions for managing water resources in a changing climate.

3.3 Human Health and Vulnerability Climate change poses risks to human health, particularly among vulnerable populations. We will explore the impacts of heatwaves, extreme weather events, changing disease patterns, and air pollution on public health. Furthermore, we will discuss the socioeconomic and demographic factors that contribute to differential vulnerability and the need for adaptive strategies.

Conclusion

Understanding climate change and its impacts is essential for developing effective policies and strategies to address this global challenge. In this section, we have explored the scientific foundations of climate change, including the greenhouse effect and its causes. We have examined the profound impacts on ecosystems, including biodiversity loss, habitat disruption, and ocean acidification. Additionally, we have analyzed the socioeconomic implications, such as food security, water availability, and human health. By comprehending the intricacies of climate change, we can lay the groundwork for informed decision-making and proactive measures to mitigate its effects.

International Climate Agreements and Commitments

This section focuses on the intersection of climate change and environmental politics. In this section, we will delve into the significance of international climate agreements and commitments in addressing the global challenge of climate change. By examining key agreements, their historical context, and their effectiveness, we can understand the role of international cooperation in mitigating climate change.

1. The Evolution of International Climate Agreements

1.1 The United Nations Framework Convention on Climate Change (UNFCCC) We will explore the establishment of the UNFCCC as the primary international framework for addressing climate change. This section will discuss the key objectives, principles, and guiding mechanisms of the convention, emphasizing the importance of global cooperation and the principle of common but differentiated responsibilities.

1.2 The Kyoto Protocol We will examine the Kyoto Protocol, the first legally binding international agreement on climate change. This section will analyze the adoption, targets, and mechanisms of the protocol, including emissions reductions and carbon market mechanisms. The challenges and lessons learned from the Kyoto Protocol will be discussed, providing insights into the complexities of international climate agreements.

1.3 The Paris Agreement We will focus on the historic Paris Agreement, adopted in 2015, which aims to limit global temperature rise well below 2 degrees Celsius above pre-industrial levels. This section will discuss the key elements of the agreement, such as Nationally Determined Contributions (NDCs), transparency mechanisms, adaptation, and financial support. We will examine the significance of the Paris Agreement in strengthening global cooperation and the challenges of implementation.

2. Key International Climate Agreements and Commitments

2.1 Nationally Determined Contributions (NDCs) We will explore the concept of NDCs, which are voluntary commitments made by countries to reduce their greenhouse gas emissions and adapt to the impacts of climate change. This section will analyze the process of formulating and updating NDCs, the diversity of targets and actions, and the role of transparency in tracking progress.

2.2 Global Climate Funds and Financial Commitments We will examine international climate finance mechanisms, such as the Green Climate Fund and other financial commitments made by developed countries. This section will discuss the importance of financial support for developing countries to mitigate and adapt to climate change, and the challenges in mobilizing and allocating climate funds.

2.3 Technology Transfer and Capacity Building We will discuss the significance of technology transfer and capacity building in international climate agreements. This section will analyze the mechanisms and initiatives aimed at promoting technology transfer, knowledge sharing, and building the capacity of developing countries to address climate change. The role of international collaboration and partnerships will be highlighted.

3. Assessing the Effectiveness of International Climate Agreements

3.1 Compliance and Enforcement Mechanisms We will examine the challenges and effectiveness of compliance and enforcement mechanisms within international climate agreements. This section will discuss the role of review processes, reporting requirements, and peer pressure in promoting accountability and driving ambition among countries.

3.2 Evaluation of Emissions Reductions and Global Progress We will assess the progress made in achieving emissions reductions and global climate goals under international agreements. This section will analyze the effectiveness of various mitigation measures, the role of carbon markets, and the potential for technology innovation to accelerate progress. The challenges of tracking emissions and ensuring accuracy will be discussed.

3.3 Adaptation and Resilience Efforts We will explore the importance of adaptation and resilience efforts in international climate agreements. This section will discuss the support provided to vulnerable countries in building adaptive capacity, addressing loss and damage, and integrating climate resilience into development planning.

4. Challenges and Future Perspectives

4.1 Equity and Fairness Considerations We will discuss the challenges associated with equity and fairness in international climate agreements. This section will examine the debates surrounding the principle of common but differentiated responsibilities, the role of historical emissions, and the need to address the needs of vulnerable countries and communities.

4.2 Global Political Will and Leadership We will analyze the role of global political will and leadership in driving international climate agreements. This section will discuss the challenges of political dynamics, competing interests, and the need for sustained commitment to ambitious climate action. The role of public pressure, civil society, and youth movements will be highlighted.

4.3 Future Directions and Enhanced Ambition We will explore the future directions of international climate agreements and the need for enhanced ambition. This section will discuss the upcoming conferences, such as the Conference of the Parties (COP), and the potential for increased cooperation, innovative approaches, and strengthened commitments. The role of emerging economies and non-state actors will be examined.

Conclusion

International climate agreements and commitments are crucial in addressing the global challenge of climate change. In this section, we have examined the evolution of key agreements, such as the UNFCCC, the Kyoto Protocol, and the Paris Agreement. We have explored the significance of Nationally Determined Contributions (NDCs), climate finance, and technology transfer in promoting global cooperation. Furthermore, we have assessed the effectiveness of international agreements, evaluated progress in emissions reductions and adaptation efforts, and discussed future challenges and directions. By understanding the complexities of international climate agreements, we can work towards collective action and stronger global commitments to mitigate climate change.

Climate Policies and Strategies

Chapter 1 explores the intersection of climate change and environmental politics. In this section, we will delve into the importance of climate policies and strategies in addressing the global challenge of climate change. By examining different approaches, policy instruments, and strategies employed by governments and international organizations, we can understand the diverse range of efforts to mitigate and adapt to climate change.

1. Policy Frameworks and Approaches

1.1 National Climate Change Policies We will examine the development and implementation of national climate change policies by various countries. This section will discuss the different approaches, such as regulatory frameworks, market-based mechanisms, and sector-specific policies, that governments employ to reduce greenhouse gas emissions and promote sustainable practices.

1.2 International Cooperation and Climate Policy We will explore the role of international cooperation in shaping climate policies. This section will discuss the significance of collaborative efforts, information sharing, and policy harmonization among countries. It will also highlight the challenges and opportunities of global climate negotiations and the influence of multilateral agreements on national policy decisions.

1.3 Policy Integration and Coherence We will examine the importance of policy integration and coherence in addressing climate change. This section will discuss the need for aligning climate policies with other policy domains, such as energy, transportation, agriculture, and urban planning. It will also explore strategies for overcoming policy silos and promoting synergistic approaches.

2. Mitigation Strategies and Actions

2.1 Renewable Energy Transition We will discuss the transition to renewable energy sources as a key mitigation strategy. This section will explore the policies and incentives that promote the deployment of renewable energy technologies, such as solar, wind, hydro, and geothermal. It will also examine the challenges and opportunities associated with scaling up renewable energy infrastructure.

2.2 Energy Efficiency and Conservation We will examine the importance of energy efficiency and conservation measures in reducing greenhouse gas emissions. This section will discuss policies and initiatives aimed at promoting energy-efficient technologies, building codes, transportation efficiency, and sustainable consumption patterns. The role of public awareness and behavioral change will be highlighted.

2.3 Carbon Pricing and Market Mechanisms We will explore the use of carbon pricing and market-based mechanisms as policy instruments for mitigating climate change. This section will discuss the design and implementation of carbon taxes, emissions trading systems, and offset mechanisms. It will also analyze the effectiveness and challenges of market-based approaches in incentivizing emissions reductions.

3. Adaptation and Resilience Strategies

3.1 Vulnerability Assessment and Risk Management We will examine the importance of vulnerability assessment and risk management in adaptation strategies. This section will discuss approaches to assess climate risks, identify vulnerable communities and sectors, and develop adaptation plans. It will also explore the integration of climate adaptation into disaster risk reduction and development planning.

3.2 Nature-based Solutions and Ecosystem Services We will discuss the role of nature-based solutions and ecosystem services in enhancing climate resilience. This section will explore strategies such as ecosystem restoration, sustainable land management, and coastal protection. It will examine the benefits of nature-based approaches in reducing vulnerability and providing multiple co-benefits.

3.3 Adaptation Finance and Support We will examine the importance of adaptation finance and support, particularly for developing countries. This section will discuss the need for financial mechanisms, capacity-building initiatives, and technology transfer to enhance adaptation efforts. It will also explore the challenges of accessing and mobilizing adaptation finance at the global and local levels.

4. Just Transition and Social Equity

4.1 Just Transition Policies and Strategies We will explore the concept of a just transition, which ensures that the shift towards a low-carbon economy is socially equitable and inclusive. This section will discuss policies and strategies aimed at supporting workers and communities affected by the transition, promoting green jobs, and addressing social inequalities.

4.2 Gender and Climate Policy We will examine the gender dimensions of climate policies and strategies. This section will discuss the unique impacts of climate change on women and girls, as well as their critical role in climate action. It will explore policies that promote gender equality, women's empowerment, and the inclusion of diverse voices in decision-making processes.

4.3 Indigenous Knowledge and Climate Adaptation We will discuss the importance of incorporating indigenous knowledge and practices in climate adaptation strategies. This section will highlight the value of traditional ecological knowledge, community-based approaches, and indigenous rights in enhancing resilience and promoting sustainable resource management.

Conclusion

Climate policies and strategies play a vital role in addressing the global challenge of climate change. In this section, we have examined the various policy frameworks, approaches, and strategies employed at the national and international levels. We have explored mitigation strategies such as renewable energy transition, energy efficiency, and carbon pricing. Additionally, we have discussed adaptation and resilience strategies, including vulnerability assessment, nature-based solutions, and adaptation finance. Furthermore, we have highlighted the importance of a just transition and social equity in climate policies. By understanding the diverse range of climate policies and strategies, we can foster effective and integrated approaches to tackle climate change.

Climate Change and Security Nexus

This section explores the interplay between climate change and environmental politics. In this section, we will delve into the climate change and security nexus, examining the complex interactions between climate change and various dimensions of global security. By analyzing the impacts of climate change on human security, conflict dynamics, and geopolitical stability, we can better understand the urgency of addressing climate change as a security issue.

1. Understanding Climate Change as a Security Challenge

1.1 Defining the Climate Change and Security Nexus We will define the concept of the climate change and security nexus and its significance in the context of global security. This section will explore the multidimensional nature of security, including human security, national security, and international security, and how climate change intersects with each dimension.

1.2 Climate Change as a Threat Multiplier We will discuss how climate change acts as a threat multiplier, exacerbating existing social, economic, and political challenges. This section will analyze the ways in which climate change impacts various sectors, such as water, food, health, and migration, and how these impacts can lead to social unrest, conflicts, and displacement.

1.3 Linkages Between Climate Change and Conflict We will explore the linkages between climate change and conflict dynamics. This section will discuss how climate change-related factors, such as resource scarcity, competition over land and water, and displacement, can contribute to the outbreak and escalation of conflicts. Case studies of specific regions affected by climate-related conflicts will be examined.

2. Impacts on Human Security

2.1 Food Security and Climate Change We will discuss the impact of climate change on food security and agricultural systems. This section will explore how changing climatic patterns, extreme weather events, and changing ecosystems affect crop yields, food production, and access to nutritious food. The implications for global hunger, malnutrition, and social stability will be analyzed.

2.2 Water Security and Climate Change We will examine the relationship between climate change and water security. This section will discuss the impacts of climate change on freshwater availability, water quality, and water-related conflicts. The challenges of managing shared water resources, transboundary disputes, and the potential for cooperation will be explored.

2.3 Health Security and Climate Change We will explore the intersection of climate change and health security. This section will discuss the direct and indirect health impacts of climate change, including the spread of vector-borne diseases, heat-related illnesses, and the disruption of healthcare systems. The vulnerabilities of marginalized communities and the need for adaptation strategies in the health sector will be emphasized.

3. Geopolitical Implications and Stability

3.1 Climate Change and Migration We will discuss the relationship between climate change and migration patterns. This section will explore how climate change-induced environmental degradation, sea-level rise, and natural disasters contribute to internal and cross-border migration. The challenges of managing climate-related migration, including the protection of human rights and the role of international cooperation, will be examined.

3.2 Geopolitical Competition Over Resources We will examine the potential for geopolitical competition over natural resources exacerbated by climate change. This section will discuss the implications of resource scarcity, particularly related to water and energy, for regional tensions and conflicts. The importance of sustainable resource management, cooperation, and diplomacy will be emphasized.

3.3 Climate Change and Conflict Prevention We will explore the role of climate change in conflict prevention and peacebuilding. This section will discuss how understanding and addressing climate change-related risks can contribute to conflict prevention strategies, early warning systems, and the promotion of sustainable development. The potential for climate diplomacy and multilateral cooperation in addressing security challenges will be highlighted.

4. Addressing the Climate Change and Security Nexus

4.1 Integrated Approaches to Climate and Security We will discuss the need for integrated approaches to address the climate change and security nexus. This section will highlight the importance of incorporating climate considerations into security policies and strategies at the national and international levels. The role of interdisciplinary research, data-sharing, and risk assessment will be examined.

4.2 Building Resilience and Adaptation We will explore strategies for building resilience and adaptation in the face of climate change-related security risks. This section will discuss the importance of community-level resilience, early warning systems, and adaptive governance structures. Case studies of successful adaptation initiatives and the role of local communities will be analyzed.

4.3 Strengthening Global Cooperation We will examine the need for strengthened global cooperation to address the climate change and security nexus. This section will discuss the role of international organizations, multilateral agreements, and regional cooperation in promoting climate resilience and security. The potential for climate-related peacebuilding initiatives and the integration of climate considerations into security frameworks will be explored.

Conclusion

The climate change and security nexus presents significant challenges to global stability and human well-being. In this section, we have explored the complex interactions between climate change and various dimensions of security, including human security, conflict dynamics, and geopolitical stability. We have discussed the impacts of climate change on food security, water security, and health security, highlighting the vulnerabilities and risks they pose. Furthermore, we have examined the geopolitical implications of climate change and the potential for resource competition and conflicts. By understanding these interconnections, we can work towards integrated approaches that address the climate change and security nexus, promote resilience, and foster global cooperation for a more secure and sustainable future.

Chapter 2: Energy Policy and Transition
Global Energy Landscape and Challenges

Chapter 2 explores the topic of energy policy and transition in the context of global challenges. In this section, we will examine the global energy landscape, including the sources of energy production, consumption patterns, and the challenges associated with the current energy system. By understanding the complexities of the global energy landscape, we can identify the need for transition towards a more sustainable and resilient energy future.

1. Energy Sources and Mix

1.1 Fossil Fuels: Challenges and Limitations We will discuss the dominant role of fossil fuels, such as coal, oil, and natural gas, in the current global energy mix. This section will highlight the challenges associated with fossil fuel extraction, including environmental degradation, air pollution, and greenhouse gas emissions. The implications for climate change and the need for transitioning away from fossil fuels will be emphasized.

1.2 Renewable Energy: Potential and Growth We will explore the potential and growth of renewable energy sources, such as solar, wind, hydro, and geothermal power. This section will discuss the advancements in renewable energy technologies, their scalability, and the increasing cost competitiveness. The role of policy support and market incentives in promoting renewable energy deployment will be examined.

1.3 Nuclear Energy: Opportunities and Concerns We will examine the role of nuclear energy in the global energy landscape. This section will discuss the potential of nuclear power to contribute to low-carbon electricity generation. It will also address the concerns related to safety, waste management, and proliferation risks associated with nuclear energy, highlighting the need for robust governance frameworks.

2. Energy Consumption Patterns

2.1 Growing Energy Demand and Urbanization We will discuss the increasing energy demand driven by population growth, economic development, and urbanization. This section will explore the challenges posed by rapid urbanization, particularly in emerging economies, and the need for sustainable energy solutions to meet growing demand. The importance of energy efficiency and smart urban planning will be highlighted.

2.2 Energy Poverty and Access We will examine the issue of energy poverty and the lack of access to modern energy services in many parts of the world. This section will discuss the social and economic implications of energy poverty and the need for inclusive energy policies that prioritize universal access to clean and affordable energy. The role of decentralized and off-grid solutions will be explored.

2.3 Energy Intensive Industries and Transition We will explore the challenges associated with energy-intensive industries, such as manufacturing, transportation, and heavy industries. This section will discuss the need for energy efficiency measures, technological innovation, and the transition to low-carbon alternatives in these sectors. The potential for circular economy principles and sustainable production practices will be examined.

3. Energy Security and Geopolitical Considerations

3.1 Energy Dependence and Geopolitical Risks We will discuss the risks and vulnerabilities associated with energy dependence on a limited number of countries or regions. This section will explore the geopolitical dynamics and conflicts that can arise from competition over energy resources. The importance of diversifying energy sources, promoting energy independence, and enhancing energy security will be emphasized.

3.2 Energy Transition and Just Transitions We will examine the concept of a just transition in the context of energy policy. This section will discuss the need to ensure that the energy transition considers the social, economic, and environmental impacts on communities, workers, and regions that are reliant on fossil fuel industries. The role of inclusive policies, retraining programs, and job creation in facilitating a just transition will be explored.

3.3 Energy Cooperation and Diplomacy We will explore the importance of international energy cooperation and diplomacy in addressing global energy challenges. This section will discuss the role of energy organizations, multilateral agreements, and regional initiatives in promoting energy security, technology sharing, and market integration. The potential for collaborative approaches to advance clean energy technologies and foster sustainable energy systems will be examined.

Conclusion

The global energy landscape is undergoing significant transformations in response to the challenges of sustainability, energy security, and climate change. In this section, we have explored the sources of energy production and the need to transition away from fossil fuels towards renewable and low-carbon alternatives. We have discussed the growing energy demand, energy poverty, and the challenges faced by energy-intensive industries. Furthermore, we have examined the geopolitical considerations and the importance of energy security in a rapidly changing world. By understanding the complexities of the global energy landscape and the associated challenges, we can work towards policies and strategies that promote a sustainable, secure, and resilient energy future.

Renewable Energy and Sustainable Development

This section explores the topic of energy policy and transition in the context of global challenges. In this section, we will focus on renewable energy and its role in promoting sustainable development. We will examine the benefits of renewable energy sources, their potential for addressing environmental concerns, and their contribution to social and economic development. By understanding the importance of renewable energy in sustainable development, we can identify pathways towards a cleaner and more resilient energy future.

1. Renewable Energy Sources and Technologies

1.1 Solar Energy We will discuss solar energy as a prominent renewable energy source. This section will explore the various technologies used to harness solar power, such as photovoltaic systems and concentrated solar power. We will highlight the scalability, cost-effectiveness, and environmental benefits of solar energy, including its role in decentralization and energy access.

1.2 Wind Energy We will examine wind energy as a key contributor to the renewable energy mix. This section will discuss onshore and offshore wind farms, turbine technologies, and advancements in wind energy generation. The potential for wind power in different regions, its intermittency challenges, and its role in decarbonizing electricity generation will be explored.

1.3 Hydropower We will explore hydropower as a renewable energy source with a long history of deployment. This section will discuss conventional and pumped-storage hydropower systems, their advantages and limitations, and the importance of sustainable dam design and operation. The role of small-scale hydropower projects and the potential for innovative hydrokinetic technologies will be examined.

1.4 Biomass Energy We will discuss biomass energy as a renewable energy source derived from organic materials. This section will explore the potential of biomass for heat, electricity, and biofuel production. The challenges of sustainable biomass sourcing, the role of bioenergy in rural development, and the need for responsible land use practices will be highlighted.

1.5 Geothermal Energy We will examine geothermal energy as a renewable energy source derived from the Earth's heat. This section will discuss geothermal power plants, direct-use applications, and the potential for harnessing geothermal energy in different geological settings. The advantages of geothermal energy, such as baseload power generation and heat supply, will be explored.

2. Environmental Benefits and Climate Mitigation

2.1 Greenhouse Gas Emissions Reduction We will discuss the environmental benefits of renewable energy sources in reducing greenhouse gas emissions. This section will explore the role of renewable energy in mitigating climate change, as well as the potential for achieving deep decarbonization through a transition to renewables. The importance of phasing out fossil fuel-based electricity generation and the potential for electrification in other sectors will be emphasized.

2.2 Air Quality and Pollution Reduction We will examine the positive impact of renewable energy on air quality improvement. This section will discuss the reduction of air pollutants, such as sulfur dioxide, nitrogen oxides, and particulate matter, through the displacement of fossil fuel combustion. The potential health benefits and socioeconomic implications of cleaner air will be explored.

2.3 Biodiversity Conservation and Land Use We will explore the relationship between renewable energy development and biodiversity conservation. This section will discuss the importance of sustainable siting and design of renewable energy projects to minimize negative impacts on ecosystems and wildlife. The potential for synergies between renewable energy deployment and land use practices, such as agroforestry and restoration, will be examined.

3. Social and Economic Development

3.1 Energy Access and Universal Electricity We will discuss the role of renewable energy in promoting energy access and universal electricity. This section will examine how decentralized renewable energy systems can provide electricity to off-grid communities and remote areas, thereby bridging the energy access gap. The potential for productive uses of renewable energy in rural electrification and socioeconomic development will be explored.

3.2 Job Creation and Economic Opportunities We will explore the potential for job creation and economic opportunities through the deployment of renewable energy technologies. This section will discuss the growth of the renewable energy sector, the expansion of green jobs, and the potential for local manufacturing and supply chains. The importance of skill development and training programs to support the renewable energy workforce will be highlighted.

3.3 Energy Transition and Just Transitions We will examine the concept of a just transition in the context of renewable energy and sustainable development. This section will discuss the need to ensure that the energy transition considers the social, economic, and environmental impacts on communities, workers, and regions. The role of inclusive policies, social equity, and participatory decision-making processes will be explored.

Conclusion

Renewable energy plays a vital role in promoting sustainable development by addressing environmental challenges, mitigating climate change, and fostering social and economic progress. In this section, we have explored various renewable energy sources and technologies, highlighting their advantages and limitations. We have discussed the environmental benefits of renewable energy in terms of greenhouse gas emissions reduction, air quality improvement, and biodiversity conservation. Furthermore, we have examined the social and economic development opportunities associated with renewable energy, including energy access, job creation, and just transitions. By embracing renewable energy as a key component of our energy systems, we can advance towards a more sustainable and resilient future.

Fossil Fuel Dependency and Transition Strategies

Chapter 2 explores the topic of energy policy and transition in the context of global challenges. In this section, we will focus on the issue of fossil fuel dependency and the need for transition strategies to reduce reliance on fossil fuels. We will examine the challenges associated with fossil fuel consumption, including environmental impacts, resource depletion, and geopolitical considerations. By understanding the complexities of fossil fuel dependency and exploring transition strategies, we can pave the way for a sustainable and low-carbon energy future.

1. Fossil Fuel Dependency and Its Implications

1.1 The Dominance of Fossil Fuels in the Global Energy Mix We will discuss the historical and current dominance of fossil fuels, such as coal, oil, and natural gas, in the global energy mix. This section will explore the reasons behind their widespread use, including their energy density, availability, and infrastructure. The environmental, social, and economic implications of fossil fuel dependency will be examined.

1.2 Environmental Impacts of Fossil Fuel Consumption We will examine the environmental impacts associated with fossil fuel consumption. This section will discuss air pollution, including emissions of greenhouse gases and pollutants that contribute to climate change and local air quality issues. The environmental consequences of fossil fuel extraction, transportation, and combustion will be highlighted.

1.3 Resource Depletion and Energy Security We will explore the challenges of resource depletion and the implications for energy security. This section will discuss the finite nature of fossil fuel reserves and the potential for supply disruptions and price volatility. The concept of "peak oil" and its implications for global energy markets will be examined.

1.4 Geopolitical Considerations and Conflicts We will examine the geopolitical dynamics and conflicts that can arise from competition over fossil fuel resources. This section will discuss the implications of fossil fuel dependency on regional stability, international relations, and conflicts. The importance of diversifying energy sources and reducing geopolitical risks associated with fossil fuel dependence will be explored.

2. Transition Strategies: Moving Away from Fossil Fuels

2.1 Renewable Energy Transition We will discuss the role of renewable energy in transitioning away from fossil fuels. This section will explore the potential of renewable energy sources, such as solar, wind, hydro, and geothermal power, in replacing fossil fuel-based electricity generation. The importance of supportive policies, investment incentives, and technology advancements in facilitating the renewable energy transition will be emphasized.

2.2 Energy Efficiency and Demand Reduction We will examine the importance of energy efficiency and demand reduction as strategies to reduce fossil fuel consumption. This section will discuss energy-efficient technologies, building design, transportation systems, and industrial processes that can contribute to lowering energy demand. The potential for behavioral changes and consumer awareness in promoting energy conservation will be explored.

2.3 Carbon Capture, Utilization, and Storage (CCUS) We will discuss the role of carbon capture, utilization, and storage (CCUS) technologies in mitigating the emissions from fossil fuel-based industries. This section will explore the potential for capturing and storing carbon dioxide emissions from power plants, industrial facilities, and other sources. The challenges, opportunities, and scalability of CCUS technologies will be examined.

2.4 Transitioning the Transportation Sector We will examine the challenges and strategies for transitioning the transportation sector away from fossil fuels. This section will discuss the role of electric vehicles (EVs), fuel efficiency standards, alternative fuels, and sustainable transportation infrastructure. The potential for integrating renewable energy and electrification in the transportation sector will be explored.

3. Economic and Social Considerations

3.1 Economic Implications and Opportunities We will discuss the economic implications of transitioning away from fossil fuels. This section will explore the potential for job creation, economic diversification, and innovation in renewable energy and clean technology sectors. The importance of supporting affected workers and communities during the transition will be highlighted.

3.2 Just Transition and Social Equity We will examine the concept of a just transition in the context of fossil fuel phase-out. This section will discuss the importance of considering social equity, worker retraining, and community development in transition strategies. The potential for inclusive decision-making processes and stakeholder engagement will be explored.

3.3 Regional and International Cooperation We will discuss the importance of regional and international cooperation in facilitating a successful transition away from fossil fuels. This section will explore collaborative initiatives, policy coordination, and knowledge sharing among countries and regions. The role of international organizations and agreements in supporting transition efforts will be examined.

Conclusion

Fossil fuel dependency poses significant challenges to sustainability, environmental quality, and energy security. In this section, we have explored the implications of fossil fuel consumption, including environmental impacts, resource depletion, and geopolitical considerations. We have discussed various transition strategies, including renewable energy deployment, energy efficiency, carbon capture, and transportation sector transformation. Furthermore, we have examined the economic and social considerations of transitioning away from fossil fuels, emphasizing the importance of a just transition and regional/international cooperation. By implementing effective transition strategies, we can reduce our reliance on fossil fuels and pave the way for a sustainable and low-carbon energy future.

Role of International Cooperation in Energy Policy

This section explores the topic of energy policy and transition in the context of global challenges. In this section, we will focus on the crucial role of international cooperation in shaping and implementing effective energy policies. We will examine the need for collaboration among nations to address energy-related challenges such as climate change, energy security, and sustainable development. By understanding the role of international cooperation, we can identify opportunities for collective action and forge a more sustainable and resilient energy future.

1. Rationale for International Cooperation in Energy Policy

1.1 Interconnectedness of Energy Systems We will discuss the interconnected nature of energy systems and the recognition that energy challenges transcend national boundaries. This section will highlight the global nature of energy-related issues, such as climate change mitigation, resource depletion, and energy access. The need for collective efforts to address these challenges will be emphasized.

1.2 Climate Change and Sustainable Development Goals We will examine the critical link between energy policy, climate change, and the achievement of sustainable development goals. This section will discuss the role of international cooperation in reducing greenhouse gas emissions, promoting renewable energy deployment, and ensuring access to clean and affordable energy. The significance of aligning national energy policies with international climate commitments, such as the Paris Agreement, will be explored.

1.3 Energy Security and Geopolitical Considerations We will explore the importance of international cooperation in enhancing energy security and mitigating geopolitical risks. This section will discuss the diversification of energy sources, energy infrastructure development, and cooperation in emergency response mechanisms. The need for collaboration in ensuring reliable and resilient energy supply will be examined.

2. International Platforms and Mechanisms for Energy Cooperation

2.1 International Energy Organizations and Initiatives We will discuss prominent international organizations and initiatives that facilitate energy cooperation among nations. This section will explore the role of organizations such as the International Energy Agency (IEA), International Renewable Energy Agency (IRENA), and United Nations Framework Convention on Climate Change (UNFCCC) in promoting dialogue, knowledge exchange, and collaborative projects. The activities and achievements of these organizations will be highlighted.

2.2 Multilateral Energy Agreements and Treaties We will examine multilateral energy agreements and treaties that foster cooperation on energy-related issues. This section will discuss agreements such as the Energy Charter Treaty, the Clean Energy Ministerial, and regional energy cooperation frameworks. The significance of these agreements in promoting policy coordination, technology transfer, and investment facilitation will be explored.

2.3 Financial and Technological Cooperation We will explore the importance of financial and technological cooperation in energy policy. This section will discuss mechanisms for technology transfer, research collaboration, and capacity-building support. The role of international financial institutions, climate funds, and public-private partnerships in mobilizing resources for clean energy projects will be examined.

3. Areas of International Cooperation in Energy Policy

3.1 Renewable Energy Deployment and Integration We will discuss the role of international cooperation in promoting renewable energy deployment and integration. This section will explore collaborative efforts in sharing best practices, harmonizing standards, and supporting renewable energy projects. The potential for cross-border renewable energy trade and interconnection will be highlighted.

3.2 Energy Efficiency and Conservation We will examine international cooperation in promoting energy efficiency and conservation. This section will discuss initiatives aimed at sharing energy-saving technologies, implementing energy efficiency standards, and promoting energy management practices. The role of international partnerships in raising awareness, conducting capacity-building activities, and supporting policy implementation will be explored.

3.3 Energy Access and Universal Electricity We will explore international cooperation in improving energy access and achieving universal electricity. This section will discuss collaborative efforts in extending electricity grids, promoting off-grid solutions, and supporting energy access in developing countries. The role of partnerships, financial mechanisms, and technological innovation in bridging the energy access gap will be examined.

4.   Overcoming   Challenges   and   Enhancing Cooperation

4.1 Political Will and Policy Alignment We will discuss the importance of political will and policy alignment among nations to foster effective international cooperation in energy policy. This section will explore the challenges associated with diverse national interests, policy priorities, and governance structures. The potential for diplomatic engagement, peer pressure, and shared objectives to overcome these challenges will be examined.

4.2 Technology Transfer and Capacity Building We will examine the need for technology transfer and capacity-building support to enhance international cooperation. This section will discuss the barriers to technology transfer, intellectual property rights, and the role of capacity building in enabling developing countries to participate effectively in energy cooperation initiatives. The importance of knowledge sharing, training programs, and technical assistance will be highlighted.

4.3 Financial Mechanisms and Investment Facilitation We will explore the role of financial mechanisms and investment facilitation in enhancing international cooperation in energy policy. This section will discuss the challenges of mobilizing financial resources for clean energy projects, attracting private sector investment, and ensuring a fair distribution of financial benefits. The potential for innovative financing instruments, risk mitigation mechanisms, and blended finance approaches will be examined.

Conclusion

International cooperation is essential in addressing global energy challenges and shaping effective energy policies. In this section, we have explored the rationale for international cooperation, focusing on climate change, energy security, and sustainable development goals. We have discussed the role of international platforms, mechanisms, and agreements in facilitating energy cooperation among nations. Furthermore, we have examined specific areas of international cooperation, including renewable energy deployment, energy efficiency, and energy access. By enhancing international cooperation in energy policy, we can leverage collective expertise, resources, and efforts to

accelerate the transition to a sustainable and resilient energy
future.

Chapter 3: Rising Powers: India
India's Growing Influence in Global Politics

Chapter 3 focuses on the rising power of India and its evolving role in global politics. In this section, we will explore the factors that contribute to India's increasing influence on the global stage. We will analyze India's economic growth, diplomatic engagement, and regional partnerships, highlighting the implications of its rise for global politics. By understanding India's growing influence, we can gain insights into the changing dynamics of the international system and the potential for cooperation and collaboration.

1. Economic Growth and Transformation

1.1 India's Economic Rise We will examine India's remarkable economic growth and transformation over the past few decades. This section will discuss the factors driving India's economic success, such as market liberalization, investment in infrastructure, and the emergence of a vibrant entrepreneurial ecosystem. The role of sectors such as information technology, manufacturing, and services in India's economic expansion will be explored.

1.2 Implications for Global Economy We will analyze the implications of India's economic growth for the global economy. This section will discuss India's position as one of the world's fastest-growing major economies and its potential as a driver of global economic growth. The impact of India's consumer market, skilled workforce, and increasing economic integration on global trade, investment, and supply chains will be examined.

1.3 Challenges and Opportunities We will explore the challenges and opportunities that accompany India's economic growth. This section will discuss issues such as income inequality, poverty alleviation, and sustainable development. The potential for India to leverage its economic power for regional and global development initiatives will be examined, including initiatives such as the International Solar Alliance and the Coalition for Disaster Resilient Infrastructure.

2. Political System and Democratic Governance

2.1 India's Democratic Governance We will examine India's democratic system and its implications for its global influence. This section will discuss the strengths and challenges of India's democratic governance, including its diversity, political pluralism, and the role of institutions. The impact of India's democratic values and practices on its foreign policy and diplomatic engagements will be analyzed.

2.2 Soft Power and Cultural Influence We will explore India's soft power and cultural influence on the global stage. This section will discuss India's rich history, traditions, and contributions to art, literature, music, and cinema. The global appeal of Indian culture, including yoga, Ayurveda, and Bollywood, and its role in shaping India's image and enhancing its diplomatic engagements will be examined.

2.3 Indian Diaspora and People-to-People Connections We will analyze the role of the Indian diaspora in India's growing influence in global politics. This section will discuss the significant Indian diaspora spread across various countries and their contributions to host countries and their homeland. The potential of people-to-people connections, cultural exchanges, and diaspora networks in fostering India's diplomatic relations and economic partnerships will be explored.

3. Regional and International Relations

3.1 India's Neighborhood Policy We will examine India's approach to its regional neighbors and its neighborhood policy. This section will discuss India's efforts to enhance regional integration, promote stability, and address security challenges in South Asia. The impact of India's relations with countries such as Bangladesh, Sri Lanka, Nepal, and Bhutan on its regional influence will be analyzed.

3.2 India's Engagement with Major Powers We will explore India's engagement with major powers and its implications for global politics. This section will discuss India's strategic partnerships and engagements with countries such as the United States, Russia, China, and European nations. The role of these relationships in shaping India's foreign policy, addressing global challenges, and expanding its influence will be examined.

3.3 India's Multilateral Engagements We will analyze India's participation in multilateral forums and its contributions to global governance. This section will discuss India's engagement with organizations such as the United Nations, BRICS, G20, and the World Trade Organization. The role of India in shaping global agendas, addressing global challenges, and promoting global cooperation will be examined.

4. Implications and Future Perspectives

4.1 Geopolitical Implications We will discuss the geopolitical implications of India's growing influence in global politics. This section will analyze the impact of India's rise on the regional balance of power, its implications for major power relations, and the potential for cooperation or competition. The challenges and opportunities arising from India's rise in a multipolar world will be examined.

4.2 India's Role in Global Challenges We will explore India's role in addressing global challenges such as climate change, sustainable development, and security. This section will discuss India's commitments under international agreements, its efforts in renewable energy deployment, and its contributions to peacekeeping operations. The potential for India to play a greater role in global governance and shaping the global agenda will be examined.

4.3 Future Perspectives We will conclude by presenting future perspectives on India's growing influence in global politics. This section will discuss the potential trajectories of India's rise, its challenges in maintaining momentum, and the implications for global stability and cooperation. The role of India's leadership, domestic reforms, and its engagement with the international community in shaping its future trajectory will be explored.

Conclusion

India's growing influence in global politics is a significant development in the changing dynamics of the international system. In this section, we have examined the factors contributing to India's rise, including its economic growth, democratic governance, and regional and international engagements. We have analyzed the implications of India's influence on the global economy, its soft power and cultural influence, and its role in regional and global affairs. By understanding India's growing influence, we can better comprehend the opportunities and challenges it presents for global politics and the potential for collaboration and cooperation on global challenges.

Political System and Democratic Governance

This section focuses on India's rising power and its political system, highlighting the significance of democratic governance in shaping its domestic and international affairs. In this section, we will delve into the structure of India's political system, the principles of democratic governance, and their impact on India's political landscape. By understanding India's political system and democratic governance, we can gain insights into the country's governance practices, decision-making processes, and the role of institutions in shaping its rise as a global power.

1. Overview of India's Political System

1.1 Constitutional Framework We will provide an overview of India's constitutional framework, highlighting the key features that define its political system. This section will discuss the adoption of the Indian Constitution, the separation of powers, and the checks and balances in place to safeguard democratic governance. The significance of fundamental rights, the rule of law, and the independence of the judiciary will be examined.

1.2 Federal Structure and Governance We will explore the federal structure of India's political system, including the division of powers between the central government and the states. This section will discuss the role of the President, the Prime Minister, and the Council of Ministers in the central government, as well as the Chief Ministers and State Assemblies at the state level. The dynamics of intergovernmental relations and cooperative federalism will be analyzed.

1.3 Political Parties and Electoral System We will analyze the role of political parties and the electoral system in India's political landscape. This section will discuss the multiparty system, the emergence of national and regional parties, and their influence on policy-making and governance. The functioning of the Election Commission, the process of elections, and the significance of voter participation will be examined.

2. Principles of Democratic Governance

2.1 Representation and Participation We will explore the principles of representation and participation in India's democratic governance. This section will discuss the importance of inclusive and accountable governance, ensuring the representation of diverse interests, and the participation of citizens in decision-making processes. The role of political institutions, civil society organizations, and media in promoting democratic values and fostering public engagement will be examined.

2.2 Rule of Law and Human Rights We will analyze the principles of the rule of law and the protection of human rights in India's democratic governance. This section will discuss the significance of an independent judiciary, the enforcement of laws, and the protection of individual liberties and freedoms. The challenges and progress in upholding human rights, addressing social justice, and promoting equality will be examined.

2.3 Transparency and Accountability We will explore the principles of transparency and accountability in India's democratic governance. This section will discuss mechanisms such as the Right to Information Act, anti-corruption measures, and the role of oversight institutions in ensuring transparency and accountability in public administration. The challenges of corruption, political finance, and the promotion of ethical governance will be analyzed.

3. Challenges and Dynamics of India's Political System

3.1 Diversity and Pluralism We will discuss the challenges and dynamics arising from India's diversity and pluralism. This section will examine the complexities of managing a diverse country with multiple languages, religions, and cultural traditions. The role of political consensus-building, social cohesion, and inclusive policies in managing diversity and promoting national integration will be explored.

3.2 Decentralization and Local Governance We will analyze the challenges and potential of decentralization and local governance in India. This section will discuss the role of Panchayati Raj institutions and urban local bodies in grassroots democracy, service delivery, and participatory governance. The importance of empowering local communities, promoting citizen engagement, and ensuring effective implementation of policies will be examined.

3.3 Gender Representation and Empowerment We will examine the dynamics of gender representation and empowerment in India's political system. This section will discuss the challenges faced by women in accessing political power and the efforts made to enhance their political participation. The role of affirmative action, women's reservation in local governance, and the need for gender-responsive policies will be explored.

Conclusion

India's political system and democratic governance play a crucial role in shaping its domestic stability and international standing as a rising power. In this section, we have explored the constitutional framework, federal structure, and electoral system that define India's political system. We have discussed the principles of democratic governance, including representation, participation, rule of law, and transparency. Furthermore, we have examined the challenges and dynamics of India's political system, such as diversity, decentralization, and gender empowerment. By understanding India's political system and democratic governance, we can gain valuable insights into the factors shaping its rise as a global power and the potential for cooperation and collaboration on global challenges.

Economic Development and Challenges

Chapter 3 focuses on India's rising power and examines various aspects of its development trajectory. This section will delve into India's economic growth, the challenges it faces, and the impact of its economic development on domestic and international dynamics. By understanding India's economic development and challenges, we can gain insights into the factors shaping its rise as a global power and its potential contributions to global stability and cooperation.

1. Economic Growth and Transformation

1.1 Overview of India's Economic Growth We will provide an overview of India's economic growth, highlighting key milestones and transformations. This section will discuss the phases of economic development, from the pre-reform era to the liberalization and globalization period. The factors driving India's economic growth, including demographic dividend, technological advancements, and market reforms, will be examined.

1.2 Sectors Driving Economic Growth We will analyze the sectors that have contributed significantly to India's economic growth. This section will discuss the role of agriculture, industry, and services sectors, and their respective contributions to the national economy. The emergence of knowledge-based industries, digital innovation, and the service sector's increasing share in GDP will be explored.

1.3 Foreign Direct Investment and Trade We will examine the role of foreign direct investment (FDI) and international trade in India's economic development. This section will discuss the trends in FDI inflows, trade patterns, and the government's initiatives to attract foreign investment. The challenges and opportunities arising from India's integration into global value chains and its trade relations with major economies will be analyzed.

2. Challenges in Economic Development

2.1 Poverty and Inequality We will explore the challenges of poverty and inequality in India's economic development. This section will discuss the efforts made to alleviate poverty through poverty reduction programs, social welfare schemes, and inclusive growth strategies. The persisting challenges of income disparity, regional disparities, and social exclusion will be examined.

2.2 Infrastructure Development We will analyze the challenges and opportunities in India's infrastructure development. This section will discuss the importance of robust infrastructure, including transportation, energy, and digital connectivity, in supporting economic growth. The initiatives taken to address infrastructure gaps, promote public-private partnerships, and enhance connectivity will be examined.

2.3 Unemployment and Skill Development We will examine the challenges of unemployment and the need for skill development in India. This section will discuss the employment generation potential of various sectors, the skills gap, and the initiatives taken to enhance employability through skill development programs. The role of entrepreneurship, innovation, and job creation in India's economic development will be explored.

3. Sustainable Development and Environmental Considerations

3.1 Environmental Challenges We will discuss the environmental challenges associated with India's economic development. This section will examine the impacts of industrialization, urbanization, and resource extraction on the environment. The challenges of air and water pollution, deforestation, and climate change will be analyzed, along with the government's efforts to address these challenges.

3.2 Sustainable Development Initiatives We will explore the sustainable development initiatives undertaken by India. This section will discuss the promotion of renewable energy, conservation of natural resources, and the integration of sustainability principles in policy-making. The role of public awareness, technological innovation, and international cooperation in achieving sustainable development goals will be examined.

3.3 Inclusive Growth and Social Welfare We will analyze the efforts to achieve inclusive growth and social welfare in India. This section will discuss the initiatives to uplift marginalized communities, provide social protection, and improve access to education, healthcare, and basic amenities. The challenges of inclusive development, social empowerment, and reducing disparities will be explored.

Conclusion

India's economic development journey has positioned it as a rising power with significant potential on the global stage. In this section, we have explored India's economic growth and transformation, highlighting the sectors driving its growth and the role of FDI and trade. We have also examined the challenges in economic development, including poverty and inequality, infrastructure development, unemployment, and environmental considerations. Additionally, we have discussed sustainable development initiatives, inclusive growth, and social welfare efforts. By understanding India's economic development and challenges, we can gain valuable insights into the factors shaping its rise as a global power and its potential contributions to global stability and cooperation.

India's Role in Regional and International Relations

This section explores India's rising power status and its engagement in regional and international relations. This section focuses on India's diplomatic strategies, foreign policy priorities, and its role in promoting regional stability and global cooperation. By understanding India's regional and international relations, we can gain insights into the factors shaping its rise as a global power and its contributions to regional integration, peace, and cooperation.

1. India's Foreign Policy: Priorities and Principles

1.1 Nehruvian Legacy and Non-Alignment We will examine India's foreign policy principles, with a particular focus on the Nehruvian legacy and the non-aligned movement. This section will discuss India's commitment to sovereignty, independence, and non-interference, as well as its pursuit of strategic autonomy in international relations. The relevance of non-alignment in contemporary global politics will be analyzed.

1.2 Foreign Policy Shifts and Engagements We will analyze the shifts in India's foreign policy approach over the years. This section will discuss the evolution of India's strategic partnerships, its engagement with major powers, and the expansion of diplomatic ties with emerging economies. The importance of economic diplomacy, diaspora engagement, and Track-II diplomacy will be explored.

1.3 Regional Priorities and Neighborhood First Policy We will examine India's regional priorities, with a specific focus on its "Neighborhood First" policy. This section will discuss India's engagement with South Asian Association for Regional Cooperation (SAARC), the Bay of Bengal Initiative for Multi-Sectoral Technical and Economic Cooperation (BIMSTEC), and other regional organizations. The challenges and opportunities in fostering regional cooperation and addressing regional conflicts will be analyzed.

2. India's Engagement in South Asia

2.1 India-Pakistan Relations We will analyze the complexities of India-Pakistan relations and their impact on regional stability. This section will discuss the challenges in resolving bilateral disputes, promoting dialogue, and managing cross-border tensions. The role of terrorism, Kashmir issue, and Track-II diplomacy in India-Pakistan relations will be examined.

2.2 India-China Relations We will examine the dynamics of India-China relations and their implications for regional and global politics. This section will discuss the border disputes, economic cooperation, and the pursuit of a balanced approach in India's engagement with China. The opportunities for collaboration and the challenges in managing strategic competition will be explored.

2.3 India's Engagement with other South Asian Countries We will explore India's engagement with other

South Asian countries, including Bangladesh, Sri Lanka, Nepal, Bhutan, and the Maldives. This section will discuss the priorities, challenges, and opportunities in India's bilateral relations, economic cooperation, and cultural exchanges with these countries. The role of connectivity projects, people-to-people interactions, and regional integration efforts will be examined.

3. India's Engagement in the Indo-Pacific Region

3.1 India's Act East Policy We will examine India's Act East policy, which aims to deepen its engagement with countries in the Indo-Pacific region. This section will discuss India's strategic partnerships with countries like Japan, Australia, and the United States, and its participation in forums such as the Quad. The significance of maritime security, trade connectivity, and freedom of navigation in India's regional engagement will be analyzed.

3.2 Regional Security and Cooperation We will analyze India's role in promoting regional security and cooperation in the Indo-Pacific. This section will discuss India's participation in regional security dialogues, joint military exercises, and counter-terrorism efforts. The challenges of maritime disputes, non-traditional security threats, and the potential for building regional architecture will be examined.

4. India's Role in Global Governance

4.1 United Nations and Multilateralism We will explore India's engagement in the United Nations (UN) and its commitment to multilateralism. This section will discuss India's contributions to peacekeeping operations, its aspirations for a permanent seat in the UN Security Council, and its participation in UN initiatives such as Sustainable Development Goals (SDGs). The challenges and opportunities in global governance reforms will be analyzed.

4.2 Climate Change and Sustainable Development We will examine India's role in addressing global challenges such as climate change and sustainable development. This section will discuss India's commitments under international agreements, its efforts to promote renewable energy, and its role in global climate negotiations. The challenges of balancing economic development with environmental sustainability will be explored.

4.3 Development Cooperation and South-South Cooperation We will analyze India's development cooperation initiatives and its engagement in South-South cooperation. This section will discuss India's contributions to capacity building, technical assistance, and infrastructure development in developing countries. The potential for strengthening cooperation with other emerging powers and the challenges in balancing national interests with global responsibilities will be examined.

Conclusion

India's regional and international relations play a crucial role in shaping its rise as a global power. In this section, we have explored India's foreign policy priorities, its engagements in South Asia and the Indo-Pacific region, and its role in global governance. By understanding India's regional and international relations, we can gain valuable insights into the factors shaping its rise as a global power and its contributions to regional stability, cooperation, and global challenges.

Chapter 4: Rising Powers: Brazil
Political Landscape and Democratic Institutions

Chapter 4 explores Brazil as a rising power and examines its political landscape and democratic institutions. This section delves into Brazil's political system, the evolution of its democratic institutions, and the challenges and opportunities they present. By understanding Brazil's political landscape and democratic governance, we can gain insights into its role as a global player and its contributions to regional and international cooperation.

1. Historical Overview of Brazil's Political Landscape

1.1 Colonial and Imperial Periods We will explore the historical foundations of Brazil's political landscape, including its colonial and imperial periods. This section will discuss the influence of Portuguese colonization, the transition from monarchy to republic, and the early stages of democracy in Brazil.

1.2 Military Dictatorship and the Return to Democracy We will analyze Brazil's period of military dictatorship from 1964 to 1985 and its impact on the country's political landscape. This section will discuss the challenges faced during the transition to democracy, the reestablishment of democratic institutions, and the consolidation of democratic governance in Brazil.

2. Political System of Brazil

2.1 Presidential System and Separation of Powers We will examine Brazil's presidential system of government and the separation of powers between the executive, legislative, and judicial branches. This section will discuss the role and responsibilities of each branch and the checks and balances that exist within the system.

2.2 Federalism and Subnational Governance We will explore Brazil's federal system of government and the significance of subnational governance. This section will discuss the distribution of powers between the federal government and the states, the role of governors and mayors, and the challenges and opportunities in subnational governance.

2.3 Political Parties and Electoral System We will analyze Brazil's political party system and the electoral system. This section will discuss the major political parties, their ideologies, and their role in the political landscape. The electoral process, campaign financing, and the challenges of political representation will be explored.

3. Democratic Institutions in Brazil

3.1 The Constitution and Rule of Law We will examine the Brazilian Constitution and its importance in upholding the rule of law. This section will discuss the fundamental rights and principles enshrined in the Constitution, the role of the judiciary in safeguarding democratic values, and the challenges in ensuring access to justice.

3.2 Legislative Branch and Lawmaking Process We will explore the Brazilian legislature, known as the National Congress, and the lawmaking process. This section will discuss the roles and functions of the Chamber of Deputies and the Federal Senate, the process of bill drafting and approval, and the challenges in legislative effectiveness.

3.3 Judiciary and Judicial Independence We will analyze the Brazilian judiciary and its role in upholding the rule of law and protecting individual rights. This section will discuss the structure of the judiciary, the appointment and tenure of judges, and the challenges and opportunities in ensuring judicial independence.

4. Challenges and Opportunities in Brazil's Democratic Governance

4.1 Corruption and Accountability We will discuss the challenges posed by corruption in Brazil and the efforts to enhance accountability and transparency. This section will examine high-profile corruption cases, the role of investigative agencies, and the importance of public trust in democratic institutions.

4.2 Social Inequality and Political Representation We will explore the challenges of social inequality in Brazil and its impact on political representation. This section will discuss the efforts to promote inclusivity, diversity, and gender equality in politics, and the importance of ensuring fair representation of marginalized communities.

4.3 Public Participation and Civil Society We will analyze the role of public participation and civil society in Brazil's democratic governance. This section will discuss the importance of civic engagement, activism, and the role of non-governmental organizations in shaping public policy and holding institutions accountable.

Conclusion

Brazil's political landscape and democratic institutions play a crucial role in shaping its position as a rising power. In this section, we have explored Brazil's historical journey, its political system, and the functioning of its democratic institutions. By understanding Brazil's political landscape and democratic governance, we can gain valuable insights into its contributions to regional and international cooperation, as well as the challenges and opportunities it faces in consolidating and strengthening its democratic foundations.

Economic Growth and Socioeconomic Inequality

This section explores Brazil as a rising power, focusing on its economic growth and the challenges posed by socioeconomic inequality. This section examines Brazil's economic trajectory, the factors contributing to its growth, and the persistent issue of inequality. By understanding the dynamics of economic growth and socioeconomic inequality in Brazil, we can gain insights into its developmental challenges and the implications for its domestic and international standing.

1. Historical Overview of Brazil's Economic Growth

1.1 Early Economic Development We will explore the historical foundations of Brazil's economic growth, including the early economic activities such as agriculture, mining, and the impact of colonization. This section will discuss Brazil's transition from an agrarian to an industrial economy and the policies implemented to foster economic development.

1.2 Periods of Expansion and Crisis We will analyze key periods of economic expansion and crisis in Brazil's history. This section will discuss the impact of global economic trends, such as the commodity boom and financial crises, on Brazil's economy. It will also examine the role of domestic factors, including policy choices and structural challenges.

2. Factors Contributing to Brazil's Economic Growth

2.1 Natural Resources and Agriculture We will examine the role of natural resources, including agricultural commodities and mineral wealth, in Brazil's economic growth. This section will discuss the opportunities and challenges associated with the exploitation and management of natural resources.

2.2 Industrialization and Manufacturing Sector We will analyze Brazil's industrialization process and the growth of its manufacturing sector. This section will discuss the development of key industries, technological advancements, and the challenges faced by the manufacturing sector, including competitiveness and productivity issues.

2.3 Services and the Rise of the Knowledge Economy We will explore the role of the services sector and the emergence of the knowledge economy in Brazil's economic growth. This section will discuss the expansion of services such as finance, information technology, and creative industries, and their contribution to employment and value creation.

3. Socioeconomic Inequality in Brazil

3.1 Income Inequality and Wealth Concentration We will examine the extent of income inequality and wealth concentration in Brazil. This section will discuss the Gini coefficient, poverty rates, and the factors contributing to persistent inequality, including historical legacies, limited access to quality education and healthcare, and unequal distribution of land and resources.

3.2 Regional Disparities and Urban-Rural Divide We will analyze the regional disparities and the urban-rural divide in Brazil's socioeconomic landscape. This section will discuss the concentration of economic opportunities in urban areas, rural poverty, and the challenges of promoting inclusive development across different regions.

3.3 Social Mobility and Access to Opportunities We will explore the issue of social mobility and access to opportunities in Brazil. This section will discuss the barriers faced by marginalized groups, including racial and ethnic minorities, in accessing quality education, healthcare, and employment opportunities. It will also examine the efforts to promote social inclusion and reduce inequality.

4. Policies and Strategies for Inclusive Growth

4.1 Social Welfare Programs and Poverty Alleviation We will analyze the social welfare programs implemented in Brazil to address poverty and reduce inequality. This section will discuss initiatives such as Bolsa Família, the expansion of social security, and their impact on poverty reduction and social mobility.

4.2 Education and Skill Development We will examine the importance of education and skill development in promoting inclusive growth. This section will discuss the challenges in the education system, efforts to improve access to quality education, vocational training programs, and the role of education in reducing inequality.

4.3 Taxation and Redistribution Policies We will discuss the role of taxation and redistribution policies in addressing socioeconomic inequality in Brazil. This section will examine progressive taxation, wealth taxes, and other policy measures aimed at redistributing income and wealth.

5. Implications for Brazil's Domestic and International Standing

5.1 Social Cohesion and Political Stability We will analyze the implications of socioeconomic inequality on social cohesion and political stability in Brazil. This section will discuss the challenges posed by inequality in fostering a cohesive society and the potential social and political ramifications.

5.2 Inclusive Development and Sustainable Growth We will explore the importance of inclusive development and sustainable growth for Brazil's long-term economic prosperity. This section will discuss the linkages between inclusive policies, sustainable development goals, and the potential for Brazil to become a global leader in promoting sustainable and equitable growth.

Conclusion

The issue of socioeconomic inequality poses significant challenges to Brazil's economic growth and societal well-being. In this section, we have examined the historical overview of Brazil's economic growth, the factors contributing to its development, and the persistent problem of inequality. By understanding the complexities of economic growth and socioeconomic inequality in Brazil, we can identify policy measures and strategies to promote inclusive development, reduce inequality, and enhance Brazil's domestic and international standing.

Environmental Concerns and Rainforest Preservation

Chapter 4 explores Brazil as a rising power, focusing on its environmental concerns and the preservation of the Amazon rainforest. This section delves into the significance of Brazil's environmental challenges, the unique ecological value of the Amazon rainforest, and the efforts made to ensure its preservation. By understanding Brazil's environmental concerns and rainforest preservation initiatives, we can gain insights into the complex relationship between economic development, sustainability, and global environmental responsibility.

1. The Importance of the Amazon Rainforest

1.1 Ecological Value and Biodiversity We will explore the ecological importance of the Amazon rainforest, highlighting its unparalleled biodiversity and the critical role it plays in global climate regulation. This section will discuss the rich flora and fauna found in the rainforest and the importance of its preservation for the well-being of the planet.

1.2 Indigenous Communities and Traditional Knowledge We will examine the cultural significance of the Amazon rainforest for indigenous communities and their deep connection to the land. This section will discuss the traditional knowledge and sustainable practices of indigenous peoples, emphasizing the importance of their involvement in rainforest preservation.

2. Environmental Challenges in Brazil

2.1 Deforestation and Land Use Change We will analyze the major environmental challenge of deforestation in Brazil and its impact on the Amazon rainforest. This section will discuss the drivers of deforestation, including agriculture, illegal logging, and infrastructure development, and the consequences for biodiversity loss and greenhouse gas emissions.

2.2 Illegal Wildlife Trade and Biodiversity Conservation We will examine the issue of illegal wildlife trade in Brazil and its detrimental effects on biodiversity conservation. This section will discuss the trafficking of endangered species, the impacts on ecosystems, and the efforts to combat illegal wildlife trade.

2.3 Water Resources and Sustainable Management We will explore the importance of water resources in Brazil and the challenges of sustainable management. This section will discuss issues such as water pollution, dam construction, and the need for integrated water resource management to ensure long-term sustainability.

3. Environmental Policies and Preservation Efforts

3.1 Legal Framework and Protected Areas We will analyze the legal framework for environmental protection in Brazil and the establishment of protected areas. This section will discuss key policies and laws, such as the Forest Code and Indigenous Lands, and their role in preserving the Amazon rainforest.

3.2 Monitoring and Enforcement We will examine the challenges of monitoring and enforcing environmental regulations in Brazil. This section will discuss the role of government agencies, satellite monitoring technologies, and the importance of collaboration between different stakeholders in combatting deforestation and illegal activities.

3.3 Indigenous Rights and Community-Based Conservation We will explore the role of indigenous rights and community-based conservation initiatives in rainforest preservation. This section will discuss the empowerment of indigenous communities, sustainable land management practices, and the importance of respecting indigenous rights and traditional knowledge.

4. International Collaboration and Partnerships

4.1 International Agreements and Cooperation We will analyze Brazil's engagement in international agreements and collaborations focused on environmental conservation. This section will discuss partnerships with other countries, international organizations, and initiatives such as REDD+ (Reducing Emissions from Deforestation and Forest Degradation).

4.2 Sustainable Development and Green Economy We will examine the potential for sustainable development and the transition to a green economy in Brazil. This section will discuss the integration of environmental considerations into economic policies, renewable energy initiatives, and the promotion of sustainable business practices.

5. Challenges and Future Directions

5.1 Balancing Development and Conservation We will discuss the challenges of balancing economic development and environmental conservation in Brazil. This section will examine the tensions between extractive industries, agricultural expansion, and the preservation of the Amazon rainforest, highlighting the need for sustainable development models.

5.2 Strengthening Governance and Law Enforcement We will explore the importance of strengthening governance and law enforcement mechanisms to address environmental challenges in Brazil. This section will discuss the need for transparency, accountability, and effective regulation to combat deforestation and ensure the long-term preservation of the rainforest.

5.3 Global Environmental Responsibility We will examine Brazil's role in global environmental responsibility and its impact on international climate change mitigation efforts. This section will discuss the expectations and responsibilities placed on Brazil as a rising power to contribute to global sustainability and combat climate change.

Conclusion

The preservation of the Amazon rainforest and addressing Brazil's environmental concerns are vital not only for the country but also for the global community. In this section, we have explored the ecological value of the Amazon rainforest, the environmental challenges faced by Brazil, and the efforts made to ensure its preservation. By recognizing the significance of rainforest preservation, promoting sustainable practices, and engaging in international collaborations, Brazil can play a crucial role in mitigating climate change and conserving one of the world's most valuable ecosystems.

Brazil's Engagement in Global Affairs

This section explores Brazil as a rising power and its engagement in global affairs. This section focuses on Brazil's active role in international relations, its pursuit of strategic partnerships, and its contributions to global governance. By examining Brazil's engagement in global affairs, we gain insights into its evolving foreign policy priorities and its aspirations for regional and global leadership.

1. Historical Overview of Brazil's Foreign Policy

1.1 Independence and Regional Influence We will provide a historical overview of Brazil's foreign policy, highlighting its emergence as an independent nation and its efforts to assert regional influence. This section will discuss Brazil's early diplomatic engagements and its pursuit of peaceful coexistence with neighboring countries.

1.2 Democratization and Diplomatic Activism We will examine Brazil's diplomatic transformation during the democratization process and its increasing diplomatic activism on the global stage. This section will discuss Brazil's participation in multilateral organizations, such as the United Nations, and its role in promoting democratic values and human rights.

2. Strategic Partnerships and Regional Integration

2.1 South-South Cooperation and BRICS We will analyze Brazil's engagement in South-South cooperation and its participation in the BRICS (Brazil, Russia, India, China, South Africa) grouping. This section will discuss the objectives, achievements, and challenges of these partnerships in fostering economic development and global multipolarity.

2.2 Mercosur and Regional Integration We will explore Brazil's involvement in Mercosur (Southern Common Market) and its commitment to regional integration in South America. This section will discuss the benefits, tensions, and future prospects of Mercosur as a mechanism for economic cooperation and political dialogue.

3. Brazil's Role in Global Governance

3.1 United Nations and Peacekeeping Operations We will examine Brazil's contributions to the United Nations and its involvement in peacekeeping operations. This section will discuss Brazil's commitment to international security, peacebuilding efforts, and its role in conflict resolution initiatives.

3.2 Environmental Diplomacy and Climate Change We will analyze Brazil's engagement in environmental diplomacy and its role in global efforts to combat climate change. This section will discuss Brazil's participation in international climate negotiations, its commitment to sustainable development, and its contributions to the preservation of the Amazon rainforest.

3.3 Trade and Economic Diplomacy We will explore Brazil's trade and economic diplomacy, focusing on its pursuit of bilateral and multilateral trade agreements. This section will discuss Brazil's role in promoting fair trade practices, its engagement in global trade forums, and its efforts to enhance economic cooperation with various regions.

4. Regional Leadership and Mediation Efforts

4.1 Leadership in South America We will examine Brazil's aspirations for regional leadership in South America and its role in mediating regional conflicts. This section will discuss Brazil's diplomatic initiatives, its involvement in regional organizations like UNASUR (Union of South American Nations), and its efforts to promote stability and cooperation in the region.

4.2 Mediation in International Conflicts We will explore Brazil's engagement in international conflict mediation efforts beyond its regional sphere of influence. This section will discuss Brazil's participation in mediation initiatives, its contributions to peace processes, and its commitment to upholding the principles of non-intervention and sovereignty.

5. Challenges and Future Directions

5.1 Economic Diplomacy and Market Access We will discuss the challenges Brazil faces in expanding its economic diplomacy and gaining increased market access. This section will examine the barriers to trade and investment, the need for structural reforms, and the strategies Brazil can employ to enhance its global economic engagement.

5.2 Balancing National Interests and Global Responsibilities We will analyze the challenges Brazil faces in balancing its national interests with its global responsibilities. This section will explore the tensions between domestic priorities and international commitments, and the implications for Brazil's engagement in global affairs.

Conclusion

In conclusion, Brazil's engagement in global affairs reflects its evolving foreign policy, regional leadership aspirations, and commitment to addressing global challenges. By actively participating in international organizations, fostering strategic partnerships, and contributing to global governance, Brazil seeks to shape regional and global agendas. However, it also faces various challenges in navigating the complex dynamics of international relations. Understanding Brazil's engagement in global affairs provides valuable insights into its role as a rising power and its potential to contribute to global stability, cooperation, and sustainable development.

Chapter 5: Rising Powers: Turkey
Political System and Governance Challenges

Chapter 5 explores Turkey as a rising power and examines its political system and governance challenges. This section delves into the complexities of Turkey's political landscape, highlighting its democratic institutions, governance issues, and the evolving dynamics of power. By analyzing the political system and governance challenges, we gain a comprehensive understanding of Turkey's domestic political landscape and its implications for regional and international relations.

1. Historical Overview of Turkey's Political System

1.1 From Ottoman Empire to the Republic We will provide a historical overview of Turkey's political system, tracing its roots from the Ottoman Empire to the establishment of the modern Turkish Republic. This section will discuss key milestones in Turkey's political development, including the reforms of Mustafa Kemal Atatürk and the transition to a parliamentary democracy.

1.2 Democratic Institutions and Constitutional Framework We will explore the democratic institutions and constitutional framework of Turkey, focusing on the separation of powers, the role of the president, the parliament, and the judiciary. This section will provide an overview of Turkey's political structure and the mechanisms of governance.

2. Challenges to Democracy and Rule of Law

2.1 Freedom of Expression and Press Freedom We will analyze the challenges to freedom of expression and press freedom in Turkey. This section will discuss the restrictions on media independence, the impact of censorship and self-censorship, and the implications for democratic discourse and public participation.

2.2 Human Rights and Civil Liberties We will examine the human rights situation in Turkey, discussing issues such as freedom of assembly, minority rights, and the treatment of political prisoners. This section will also address concerns related to the independence of the judiciary and the state of emergency measures.

2.3 Civil-Military Relations We will explore the dynamics of civil-military relations in Turkey and their influence on the political system. This section will discuss the historical role of the military in Turkish politics, the challenges of civilian control, and the impact on democratic governance.

3. Political Parties and Electoral Process

3.1 Party System and Political Fragmentation We will analyze Turkey's party system and the challenges posed by political fragmentation. This section will discuss the dominant political parties, the rise of new political movements, and the implications for political stability and effective governance.

3.2 Electoral Process and Fairness We will examine the electoral process in Turkey, assessing its fairness, transparency, and inclusiveness. This section will discuss issues such as gerrymandering, campaign financing, and the role of the Supreme Electoral Council in ensuring free and fair elections.

4. Ethnic and Religious Diversity

4.1 Kurdish Question and Minority Rights We will explore the challenges posed by the Kurdish question and the quest for minority rights in Turkey. This section will discuss the historical context, the impact of the Kurdish conflict on political dynamics, and the efforts towards reconciliation and inclusion.

4.2 Religious Freedom and Secularism We will analyze the complexities of religious freedom and secularism in Turkey. This section will discuss the role of Islam in public life, the tensions between secularism and religious conservatism, and the implications for democratic governance and social cohesion.

5. Role of Civil Society and Media

5.1 Civil Society Organizations and Activism We will examine the role of civil society organizations and activism in Turkey's political landscape. This section will discuss their contributions to democratic development, human rights advocacy, and their challenges in an increasingly restrictive environment.

5.2 Media Landscape and Journalism We will analyze the state of the media landscape and journalism in Turkey. This section will discuss the influence of pro-government media, the crackdown on independent journalism, and the implications for the free flow of information and democratic accountability.

6. Prospects for Political Reform and Democratization

6.1 Reform Initiatives and Obstacles We will assess the prospects for political reform and democratization in Turkey. This section will discuss the government's reform initiatives, the obstacles to meaningful change, and the role of international actors in supporting democratic development.

6.2 Implications for Regional and International Relations We will explore the implications of Turkey's political system and governance challenges for its regional and international relations. This section will discuss how domestic dynamics influence Turkey's foreign policy, its role in regional conflicts, and its engagement with international organizations.

Conclusion

In conclusion, understanding Turkey's political system and governance challenges provides valuable insights into its domestic political landscape and its role as a rising power. By examining issues related to democracy, rule of law, civil-military relations, ethnic and religious diversity, and the role of civil society, we gain a comprehensive understanding of the complexities and dynamics of Turkey's political system. Recognizing these challenges is crucial for assessing Turkey's future trajectory and its potential to

contribute to regional stability and international
cooperation.

Geopolitical Importance and Regional Dynamics

This section explores Turkey as a rising power and focuses on its geopolitical importance and regional dynamics. This section analyzes Turkey's strategic location, its historical role as a bridge between Europe and Asia, and the impact of its regional engagement on its foreign policy. Understanding the geopolitical importance and regional dynamics of Turkey provides valuable insights into its influence, challenges, and potential contributions to regional stability and global affairs.

1. Turkey's Strategic Location

1.1 Crossroads between Europe and Asia We will explore Turkey's strategic location as a bridge between Europe and Asia. This section will discuss the historical context, emphasizing Turkey's unique position as a transit hub for trade, energy transportation, and cultural exchange.

1.2 Access to Key Waterways We will examine Turkey's access to key waterways, such as the Bosporus and the Dardanelles, and their significance for maritime trade, naval presence, and regional security. This section will discuss the legal framework governing these waterways and the geopolitical implications.

2. Regional Dynamics in the Middle East

2.1 Relations with Middle Eastern Countries We will analyze Turkey's relations with Middle Eastern countries and the evolving dynamics in the region. This section will discuss Turkey's historical ties, its role in regional conflicts, and its engagement with countries such as Syria, Iraq, Iran, and the Gulf states.

2.2 Syrian Civil War and Refugee Crisis We will examine Turkey's involvement in the Syrian civil war and the resulting refugee crisis. This section will discuss Turkey's humanitarian efforts, security concerns, and the implications for regional stability and international cooperation.

2.3 Kurdish Issue and Regional Impact We will explore the Kurdish issue and its regional impact. This section will discuss Turkey's relationship with the Kurdish populations in Syria, Iraq, and Turkey itself, the implications for regional dynamics, and the challenges of balancing domestic security concerns with regional stability.

3. Relations with Europe and the European Union

3.1 Turkey-EU Relations and Accession Process We will analyze Turkey's relations with Europe and its aspirations for EU membership. This section will discuss the challenges and opportunities in Turkey's accession process, the impact of political and economic developments, and the future of Turkey-EU relations.

3.2 Migration and Border Management We will examine Turkey's role in managing migration flows, particularly as a transit country for refugees seeking entry into Europe. This section will discuss the challenges of border management, the EU-Turkey migration deal, and the implications for regional stability and cooperation.

4. Role in NATO and Transatlantic Relations

4.1 Turkey's Membership in NATO We will analyze Turkey's role as a NATO member and its contributions to the alliance. This section will discuss Turkey's strategic importance for NATO, its involvement in regional security issues, and its relationship with other NATO members.

4.2 Turkey's Relations with the United States and Russia We will examine Turkey's relations with the United States and Russia and the dynamics of its foreign policy balancing act. This section will discuss Turkey's role in regional conflicts, its cooperation and divergences with these major powers, and the implications for regional stability.

5. Energy Security and Economic Interests

5.1 Energy Transit Routes and Pipelines We will explore Turkey's role as a transit country for energy resources and the significance of its energy transit routes and pipelines. This section will discuss the geopolitical implications, the challenges in energy cooperation, and Turkey's pursuit of energy diversification.

5.2 Economic Interests and Trade Partnerships We will analyze Turkey's economic interests and its trade partnerships in the region. This section will discuss Turkey's economic ties with neighboring countries, its pursuit of regional economic integration, and the potential for economic cooperation and development.

Conclusion

Understanding the geopolitical importance and regional dynamics of Turkey provides a comprehensive view of its role as a rising power. By examining its strategic location, relations with Middle Eastern countries and Europe, involvement in regional conflicts, role in NATO, and economic interests, we gain insights into Turkey's influence, challenges, and potential contributions to regional stability and global affairs. Recognizing the complexities of regional dynamics is crucial for assessing Turkey's future trajectory and its significance in shaping the geopolitical landscape.

Identity Politics and Social Changes

Chapter 5 delves into the rising power of Turkey and explores the dynamics of identity politics and social changes within the country. This section analyzes the diverse identity landscape of Turkey, including ethnic, religious, and cultural identities, and examines the ways in which these dynamics shape the country's domestic politics, societal dynamics, and regional influence. Understanding the complexities of identity politics and social changes in Turkey provides valuable insights into the challenges, opportunities, and future prospects for the nation.

1. Ethnic and Cultural Diversity

1.1 Turkish Identity and Ethnic Composition We will explore the concept of Turkish identity and its relationship to the diverse ethnic composition within the country. This section will discuss the major ethnic groups in Turkey, including Turks, Kurds, Arabs, and others, and examine the historical context and contemporary dynamics of their interactions.

1.2 Ethnic Conflict and Peacebuilding Efforts We will analyze the ethnic conflicts and tensions that have emerged in Turkey and discuss efforts toward peacebuilding and reconciliation. This section will highlight the challenges, such as the Kurdish issue, and explore initiatives for fostering dialogue, promoting cultural diversity, and addressing grievances.

2. Religious Pluralism and Secularism

2.1 Islam and Turkish Society We will examine the role of Islam in Turkish society and its influence on politics, culture, and social norms. This section will discuss the historical context, the impact of secularism, and the challenges and debates surrounding the relationship between religion and the state.

2.2 Religious Minorities and Interfaith Relations We will explore the situation of religious minorities in Turkey, including Christians, Jews, and Alevis, and discuss the dynamics of interfaith relations. This section will address issues of religious freedom, minority rights, and efforts to foster interreligious dialogue and cooperation.

3. Gender Equality and Women's Rights

3.1 Women's Movement and Activism We will analyze the women's movement in Turkey and its role in advocating for gender equality and women's rights. This section will discuss the challenges and progress made in areas such as political representation, access to education and employment, combating violence against women, and changing societal attitudes.

3.2 Family, Tradition, and Modernization We will examine the tensions between traditional family structures and modernization in Turkish society. This section will discuss changing gender roles, generational differences, and the impact of social, cultural, and economic factors on women's empowerment and gender equality.

4. Youth, Social Media, and Activism

4.1 Youth Demographics and Political Engagement We will explore the role of youth in Turkish society, their demographic significance, and their engagement in political and social issues. This section will discuss the impact of social media, youth activism, and the challenges and opportunities for the younger generation in shaping social and political changes.

4.2 LGBTQ+ Rights and Advocacy We will examine the status of LGBTQ+ rights in Turkey and the challenges faced by the LGBTQ+ community. This section will discuss the legal framework, societal attitudes, and the efforts of advocacy groups to promote LGBTQ+ rights and inclusivity.

5. Impact on Regional Dynamics and International Relations

5.1 Identity Politics and Regional Conflicts We will analyze how identity politics within Turkey influence its regional dynamics, particularly in relation to conflicts in the Middle East. This section will discuss the role of ethnic and religious identities, the impact on foreign policy, and the challenges of balancing domestic concerns with regional stability.

5.2 Soft Power and Cultural Diplomacy We will examine the role of Turkey's cultural heritage, including its art, literature, and cuisine, in shaping its soft power and cultural diplomacy. This section will discuss how identity politics and social changes contribute to Turkey's regional influence and its relationships with neighboring countries.

Conclusion

This chapter has explored the intricate landscape of identity politics and social changes in Turkey. By examining the country's ethnic and cultural diversity, religious pluralism, gender equality, youth activism, and their impact on regional dynamics, we gain a comprehensive understanding of Turkey's domestic and international dynamics. Recognizing the complexities of identity politics is crucial for assessing Turkey's evolving role as a rising power and its potential contributions to regional stability and cooperation.

Turkey's Role in Middle Eastern Affairs and Beyond

This section explores Turkey's rising power status and its significant role in Middle Eastern affairs and beyond. This section examines Turkey's historical connections, regional ambitions, and evolving foreign policy strategies. It analyzes Turkey's engagement in regional conflicts, diplomatic initiatives, economic partnerships, and its aspirations for greater influence on the global stage. Understanding Turkey's role in Middle Eastern affairs provides valuable insights into its regional dynamics, challenges, and potential contributions to regional stability and cooperation.

1. Historical Context and Regional Identity

1.1 Ottoman Legacy and Pan-Islamism We will delve into the historical context of the Ottoman Empire and its influence on Turkey's regional identity. This section will explore the concept of pan-Islamism and its impact on Turkey's engagement in the Middle East, considering historical, cultural, and religious ties.

1.2 Modern Turkish Foreign Policy Principles We will examine the core principles of modern Turkish foreign policy, including its focus on multilateralism, non-alignment, and active diplomacy. This section will discuss Turkey's historical shift from a regional power to a more global actor and the implications for its engagement in Middle Eastern affairs.

2. Geopolitical Position and Regional Interests

2.1 Strategic Location and Security Concerns We will analyze Turkey's strategic location and its implications for regional security dynamics. This section will discuss Turkey's role as a bridge between Europe and Asia, its proximity to conflict zones, and the challenges and opportunities presented by its geographical position.

2.2 Economic Interests and Energy Resources We will explore Turkey's economic interests in the Middle East and its efforts to enhance economic cooperation and trade partnerships. This section will discuss Turkey's access to energy resources, such as oil and natural gas, and its role as a transit hub for energy pipelines.

3. Regional Conflicts and Mediation Efforts

3.1 Syrian Civil War and the Refugee Crisis We will analyze Turkey's involvement in the Syrian civil war and its impact on regional dynamics. This section will discuss Turkey's role in hosting Syrian refugees, managing the humanitarian crisis, and its efforts to shape the outcome of the conflict.

3.2 Kurdish Issue and Counterterrorism We will examine Turkey's approach to the Kurdish issue and its counterterrorism efforts. This section will discuss the challenges posed by Kurdish separatist groups, Turkey's military operations in Syria and Iraq, and the implications for regional stability.

3.3 Mediation and Diplomatic Initiatives We will explore Turkey's role as a mediator in regional conflicts, including its diplomatic efforts in the Israeli-Palestinian conflict and the Qatar-Gulf crisis. This section will analyze Turkey's approach to conflict resolution and its aspirations for regional leadership.

4. Diplomatic Relations and Alliances

4.1 Relations with Middle Eastern Countries We will examine Turkey's relations with key Middle Eastern countries, such as Saudi Arabia, Iran, Egypt, and Israel. This section will discuss the complexities of these relationships, including areas of cooperation, rivalry, and diverging interests.

4.2 NATO Membership and Transatlantic Relations We will analyze Turkey's membership in NATO and its impact on transatlantic relations. This section will discuss Turkey's role within the alliance, its regional security contributions, and the challenges it poses to consensus-building.

5. Global Ambitions and International Engagements

5.1 Turkey's Engagement with Europe We will explore Turkey's relationship with the European Union (EU) and its aspirations for EU membership. This section will discuss the challenges and opportunities for Turkey's integration into European institutions and the impact on its regional role.

5.2 African Engagement and Development Cooperation We will analyze Turkey's growing engagement with African countries, including trade partnerships, development assistance, and cultural exchanges. This section will discuss Turkey's motivations for expanding its presence in Africa and the potential implications for regional dynamics.

5.3 Soft Power and Cultural Diplomacy We will examine Turkey's use of soft power and cultural diplomacy as tools to enhance its influence in the Middle East and beyond. This section will discuss Turkey's cultural heritage, its promotion of Turkish language and culture, and the impact on its regional image.

Conclusion

The chapter concludes by summarizing Turkey's multifaceted role in Middle Eastern affairs and its ambitions to extend its influence beyond the region. Understanding Turkey's geopolitical position, regional interests, diplomatic engagements, and global aspirations is essential for comprehending the dynamics of rising powers and their implications for global stability and cooperation.

Chapter 6: Emerging Trends and Future Scenarios Technological Advancements and Disruptive Innovations

Chapter 6 explores the emerging trends and future scenarios in the intersection of technology and global challenges. This section focuses on the rapid pace of technological advancements and their potential to disrupt various sectors, shape societal transformations, and impact global stability. By examining key technological trends and their implications, we gain insights into the challenges and opportunities they present for addressing climate change, enhancing cooperation, and shaping the future of world politics.

1. The Acceleration of Technological Advancements

1.1 The Fourth Industrial Revolution We will discuss the concept of the Fourth Industrial Revolution and its key technological drivers, such as artificial intelligence, robotics, the Internet of Things, and biotechnology. This section will explore the transformative potential of these technologies and their implications for various industries.

1.2 Big Data and Analytics We will examine the increasing availability and importance of big data and analytics in shaping decision-making processes. This section will discuss the potential of data-driven insights for understanding complex global challenges, including climate change and sustainable development.

2. Disruptive Innovations and their Impacts

2.1 Renewable Energy Technologies We will explore the advancements in renewable energy technologies and their potential to revolutionize the global energy landscape. This section will discuss the role of solar, wind, hydro, and other renewable energy sources in mitigating climate change and promoting sustainable development.

2.2 Blockchain and Distributed Ledger Technology We will analyze the disruptive potential of blockchain and distributed ledger technology in various sectors, including finance, supply chain management, and governance. This section will discuss the implications of decentralized and transparent systems for enhancing trust, security, and efficiency.

2.3 Automation and the Future of Work We will examine the impact of automation on the future of work and employment. This section will discuss the potential benefits and challenges of increased automation, including job displacement, skill requirements, and the need for reskilling and upskilling.

3. Technological Solutions for Global Challenges

3.1 Climate Change Mitigation and Adaptation We will explore how technological advancements can contribute to climate change mitigation and adaptation efforts. This section will discuss innovations in clean energy, carbon capture and storage, climate modeling, and resilience-building technologies.

3.2 Sustainable Development and Resource Management We will analyze how technology can support sustainable development practices and efficient resource management. This section will discuss innovations in smart cities, circular economy models, precision agriculture, and eco-friendly transportation.

3.3 Health and Well-being We will examine the role of technology in improving global health outcomes and promoting well-being. This section will discuss advancements in telemedicine, digital health solutions, genomics, and personalized medicine.

4. Ethical and Governance Considerations

4.1 Ethical Implications of Technological Advancements We will discuss the ethical dilemmas and considerations associated with emerging technologies. This section will explore topics such as privacy, data security, algorithmic biases, and the responsible development and use of new technologies.

4.2 Governance Challenges and Regulatory Frameworks We will analyze the governance challenges posed by technological advancements and the need for robust regulatory frameworks. This section will discuss issues of data governance, international cooperation, and the role of governments, industry, and civil society in shaping responsible technological development.

5. Future Scenarios and Implications

5.1 Shifting Power Dynamics and Geopolitical Implications We will examine how technological advancements can reshape power dynamics and influence global geopolitics. This section will discuss the potential for emerging technologies to impact international relations, economic competitiveness, and military capabilities.

5.2 Digital Divide and Inequality We will explore the digital divide and its implications for global inequality. This section will discuss the challenges of ensuring equal access to technology, bridging the digital divide, and addressing disparities in digital literacy and infrastructure.

5.3 Technological Risks and Security Concerns We will analyze the potential risks and security concerns associated with emerging technologies. This section will discuss cybersecurity threats, weaponization of technologies, and the need for international cooperation to address these challenges.

Conclusion

The chapter concludes by highlighting the transformative potential of technological advancements and the need for proactive and responsible approaches to harness their benefits while mitigating their risks. Understanding the dynamics of technological innovations is crucial for policymakers, businesses, and individuals to navigate the complex terrain of global challenges and shape a sustainable and cooperative future.

Shifting Global Order and Power Redistribution

This section explores emerging trends and future scenarios that have the potential to reshape the global order and redistribute power dynamics. This section focuses on the evolving geopolitical landscape, including the rise of new powers, changing alliances, and the impact of globalization. By examining these dynamics, we gain insights into the challenges and opportunities they present for global stability, cooperation, and the future of world politics.

1. The Dynamics of Global Power

1.1 The Unipolar World Order and its Challenges We will discuss the characteristics and limitations of the unipolar world order dominated by a single superpower. This section will examine the challenges faced by the existing power structure and the emergence of alternative power centers.

1.2 Multipolarity and the Rise of New Powers We will analyze the trend of multipolarity, characterized by the rise of new global powers. This section will explore the growing influence of countries such as China, India, and Brazil, and their impact on global politics and governance.

1.3 Power Shifts in Economic and Technological Domains We will examine the shifting balance of power in economic and technological domains. This section will discuss the increasing economic influence of emerging economies, advancements in technology, and their implications for global power dynamics.

2. Geopolitical Realignment and Regional Dynamics

2.1 Changing Alliances and Strategic Partnerships We will explore the evolving alliances and strategic partnerships among nations. This section will discuss the realignment of global powers and the formation of new geopolitical blocs, highlighting their motivations and implications.

2.2 Regional Power Dynamics and Conflicts We will analyze the power dynamics and conflicts in key regions around the world. This section will examine regional rivalries, geopolitical tensions, and their potential to shape the global order.

2.3 The Role of Non-State Actors We will discuss the influence of non-state actors, such as multinational corporations, non-governmental organizations, and transnational networks, in shaping global power dynamics. This section will explore their impact on governance, decision-making processes, and global cooperation.

3. Economic Interdependence and Globalization

3.1 Globalization and its Implications We will examine the impact of globalization on the global order and power redistribution. This section will discuss the interconnectedness of economies, trade relationships, and the challenges and benefits of economic interdependence.

3.2 Economic Inequalities and Development Gaps We will explore the economic inequalities and development gaps exacerbated by the shifting global order. This section will discuss the challenges of bridging these gaps and the role of international cooperation in promoting equitable development.

4. Technological Advancements and Disruptive Innovations

4.1 Technological Innovations and their Impact on Power We will analyze the role of technological advancements in shaping power dynamics. This section will discuss how emerging technologies can empower both state and non-state actors, potentially disrupting traditional power structures.

4.2 Digitalization and the Democratization of Information We will examine the democratization of information through digitalization and its implications for power redistribution. This section will discuss how digital technologies can amplify the voices of previously marginalized actors and impact the balance of power.

5. Implications for Global Stability and Cooperation

5.1 Challenges to Global Stability We will discuss the challenges to global stability arising from the shifting global order and power redistribution. This section will explore potential conflicts, regional instabilities, and the need for effective governance mechanisms.

5.2 Opportunities for Global Cooperation We will explore the opportunities for global cooperation in the context of a shifting global order. This section will discuss the importance of multilateralism, diplomacy, and international institutions in fostering cooperation and addressing global challenges.

Conclusion

The chapter concludes by emphasizing the significance of understanding and adapting to the shifting global order and power redistribution. By recognizing emerging trends and future scenarios, policymakers and stakeholders can proactively shape the future of world politics, promote stability, and foster cooperation on global challenges.

Migration and Refugee Crisis

Chapter 6 delves into emerging trends and future scenarios that have significant implications for global stability and cooperation. This section focuses on the pressing issue of migration and the refugee crisis, examining the complex factors driving mass movements of people and the challenges they pose for governments, societies, and international cooperation. By understanding the causes and consequences of migration, we can explore effective strategies for addressing this global challenge and fostering a more inclusive and sustainable future.

1. Understanding Migration: Causes and Patterns

1.1 Drivers of Migration We will examine the multifaceted drivers of migration, including political, economic, environmental, and social factors. This section will explore how conflicts, poverty, climate change, demographic shifts, and aspirations for a better life contribute to migration flows.

1.2 Patterns of Migration We will analyze the patterns and routes of migration, including both internal and international movements. This section will discuss different types of migration, such as economic migration, forced displacement, and asylum-seeking, and highlight regional variations and trends.

2. The Refugee Crisis: Challenges and Impacts

2.1 The Global Refugee Crisis We will provide an overview of the global refugee crisis, including the scale, scope, and regional distribution of forcibly displaced populations. This section will examine the challenges faced by refugees, including access to protection, basic services, and durable solutions.

2.2 Humanitarian and Socioeconomic Impacts We will explore the humanitarian and socioeconomic impacts of the refugee crisis on host countries and communities. This section will discuss the strain on resources, infrastructure, public services, and social cohesion, highlighting both the challenges and potential benefits.

2.3 Refugee Rights and International Legal Framework We will examine the legal framework surrounding refugee rights and protection. This section will discuss international conventions, treaties, and obligations that govern the treatment of refugees and the responsibilities of states in providing asylum and assistance.

3. Migration Governance and Policy Approaches

3.1 National Approaches to Migration We will analyze different national approaches to migration governance, including policies related to border control, immigration, and integration. This section will explore the diversity of approaches and their impacts on migrants, refugees, and host communities.

3.2 International Cooperation and Migration Governance We will discuss the importance of international cooperation in addressing migration challenges. This section will examine regional and global frameworks, such as the

Global Compact for Safe, Orderly and Regular Migration, and the role of international organizations, NGOs, and civil society in facilitating collaboration.

3.3 Comprehensive Migration Policies We will explore the concept of comprehensive migration policies that address the various dimensions of migration, including protection, human rights, labor market integration, and social cohesion. This section will highlight best practices and successful case studies from different regions.

4. Managing Migration and Refugee Flows

4.1 Border Management and Security We will discuss the complexities of border management and security in the context of migration and refugee flows. This section will explore the balance between border control, humanitarian considerations, and human rights, and the challenges of managing irregular migration.

4.2 Refugee Protection and Asylum Systems We will examine the challenges and opportunities in providing effective refugee protection and asylum systems. This section will discuss the importance of fair and efficient asylum procedures, access to legal representation, and the role of resettlement and humanitarian admission programs.

4.3 Integration and Social Cohesion We will explore strategies for promoting the successful integration of migrants and refugees into host communities. This section will discuss the importance of inclusive policies, language acquisition, education, employment opportunities, and social cohesion initiatives.

5. Addressing Root Causes and Building Sustainable Solutions

5.1 Tackling the Root Causes of Migration We will examine the importance of addressing the root causes of migration, including conflict resolution, poverty alleviation, and sustainable development. This section will explore the role of international cooperation, aid, and development programs in creating conditions for people to thrive in their home countries.

5.2 Strengthening Global Partnerships We will discuss the significance of strengthening global partnerships to address the migration and refugee crisis effectively. This section will explore collaboration between countries of origin, transit, and destination, as well as partnerships with international organizations, NGOs, and the private sector.

5.3 Building Resilient Communities We will highlight the importance of building resilient communities that can respond effectively to migration and refugee challenges. This section will discuss local initiatives, community engagement, and the empowerment of migrants and refugees themselves in shaping their futures.

Conclusion

The chapter concludes by emphasizing the urgency of addressing the migration and refugee crisis through international cooperation, comprehensive policies, and sustainable solutions. By understanding the complexities of migration, respecting refugee rights, and addressing the root causes, we can build a more inclusive and resilient global society that embraces the benefits of human mobility while ensuring the well-being and dignity of all individuals.

Social Movements and Activism in the 21st Century

This section explores emerging trends and future scenarios that shape global stability and cooperation. This section focuses on social movements and activism in the 21st century, highlighting their significance in addressing global challenges, promoting social change, and shaping the future of world politics. By examining the dynamics, strategies, and impact of contemporary social movements, we can gain insights into the evolving landscape of activism and its implications for global governance and cooperation.

1. The Evolution of Social Movements

1.1 Historical Context We will provide a brief overview of the historical context of social movements, highlighting significant movements and their impact on society and politics. This section will explore the transition from traditional activism to the digital age and the rise of global connectivity.

1.2 Characteristics and Dynamics We will discuss the characteristics and dynamics of social movements in the 21st century. This section will explore the decentralized nature of movements, the role of social media and technology, and the diverse range of issues that mobilize activists worldwide.

2. The Power of Social Movements

2.1 Influence on Policy and Governance We will examine how social movements shape policy agendas and influence governance structures at various levels, from local to global. This section will highlight case studies where movements have successfully advocated for change, addressing issues such as human rights, environmental protection, and social justice.

2.2 Amplifying Marginalized Voices We will explore how social movements amplify the voices of marginalized communities and challenge power structures that perpetuate inequality and discrimination. This section will discuss intersectionality and the importance of inclusive movements that center the experiences of diverse groups.

2.3 Inspiring and Mobilizing Youth We will discuss the role of social movements in inspiring and mobilizing young people around the world. This section will highlight the youth-led movements that have emerged in recent years, addressing issues such as climate change, gun control, and racial justice.

3. Strategies and Tactics of Contemporary Movements

3.1 Digital Activism and Online Mobilization We will explore the role of digital activism and online mobilization in contemporary social movements. This section will discuss the use of social media, online platforms, and digital tools for organizing, disseminating information, and fostering global solidarity.

3.2 Nonviolent Resistance and Civil Disobedience We will examine the strategies of nonviolent resistance and civil disobedience employed by social movements. This section will explore the theories and practices of nonviolent action, highlighting successful examples and the ethical considerations involved.

3.3 Coalition Building and Transnational Solidarity We will discuss the importance of coalition building and transnational solidarity among social movements. This section will explore how movements collaborate across borders, share resources and knowledge, and amplify their impact through collective action.

4. Challenges and Opportunities

4.1 Repression and State Responses We will address the challenges faced by social movements, including repression, surveillance, and state responses. This section will examine the strategies employed by governments to suppress activism and the implications for democratic governance and human rights.

4.2 Inclusivity and Intersectionality We will discuss the importance of inclusivity and intersectionality in social movements. This section will explore the need for movements to address multiple dimensions of oppression, embrace diversity, and foster inclusive spaces for marginalized voices.

4.3 Sustainability and Long-Term Impact We will explore the sustainability of social movements and their long-term impact on societal change. This section will discuss the challenges of sustaining momentum, translating activism into lasting policy change, and avoiding co-optation or dilution of movement goals.

5. Future Scenarios and Implications

5.1 Emerging Trends in Activism We will analyze emerging trends in activism, including new forms of organizing, the impact of technology, and the evolving strategies employed by movements. This section will explore the potential implications of these trends for future social change and political dynamics.

5.2 Influence on Global Stability and Cooperation We will discuss the influence of social movements on global stability and cooperation. This section will examine how movements can shape international agendas, influence intergovernmental organizations, and foster cross-border collaboration on pressing global challenges.

5.3 The Role of Governments and Institutions We will explore the relationship between social movements and governments or institutional actors. This section will discuss how governments and institutions respond to the demands and pressures generated by social movements and the potential for collaboration or conflict.

Conclusion

The chapter concludes by emphasizing the transformative power of social movements in the 21st century. By engaging in collective action, raising awareness, and advocating for change, social movements play a crucial role in shaping the future of world politics, addressing global challenges, and promoting a more just and sustainable world. Understanding the dynamics and impact of contemporary activism is essential for individuals, governments, and international institutions seeking to navigate the complex landscape of global governance and cooperation.

Chapter 7: Global Stability and Cooperation
The Role of International Organizations in Maintaining Stability

Chapter 7 examines the critical role of international organizations in maintaining global stability and promoting cooperation. As the world faces numerous challenges, ranging from climate change to conflict resolution, international organizations serve as crucial platforms for fostering dialogue, facilitating coordination, and addressing global issues collectively. This section explores the functions, strengths, and limitations of international organizations in promoting stability and cooperation among nations.

1. The Significance of International Organizations

1.1 Understanding International Organizations We provide an overview of international organizations, including their formation, structures, and objectives. This section highlights the diverse range of organizations operating at regional and global levels and their unique mandates.

1.2 The Evolution of International Organizations We examine the historical development of international organizations, tracing their evolution from early diplomatic forums to modern-day multilateral institutions. This section emphasizes key milestones and transformative moments that have shaped their roles in global governance.

2. Maintaining Peace and Security

2.1 The United Nations and Collective Security We discuss the United Nations (UN) as the primary international organization responsible for maintaining peace and security. This section explores the UN Security Council, peacekeeping operations, and the role of regional organizations in conflict prevention and resolution.

2.2 Arms Control and Non-Proliferation We examine the efforts of international organizations in promoting arms control, disarmament, and non-proliferation. This section highlights the role of organizations such as the International Atomic Energy Agency (IAEA) and the Organization for the Prohibition of Chemical Weapons (OPCW) in reducing global security threats.

2.3 Counterterrorism and Transnational Crime We explore the role of international organizations in combating terrorism and transnational crime. This section focuses on organizations such as INTERPOL and the Global Counterterrorism Forum (GCTF) in coordinating efforts, sharing intelligence, and fostering international cooperation.

3. Promoting Sustainable Development

3.1 The United Nations Sustainable Development Goals (SDGs) We discuss the UN's Sustainable Development Goals as a framework for addressing global challenges related to poverty, inequality, climate change, and more. This section explores the role of international organizations in implementing and monitoring progress toward the SDGs.

3.2 Environmental Protection and Conservation We examine international organizations dedicated to environmental protection and conservation. This section discusses the United Nations Environment Programme (UNEP), the Intergovernmental Panel on Climate Change (IPCC), and other bodies involved in mitigating climate change, preserving biodiversity, and promoting sustainable resource management.

3.3 Economic Cooperation and Trade We explore the role of international organizations in promoting economic cooperation and facilitating international trade. This section focuses on institutions such as the World Trade Organization (WTO), the International Monetary Fund (IMF), and regional economic organizations in fostering economic stability and integration.

4. Human Rights and Social Justice

4.1 The Role of Human Rights Organizations We discuss the contributions of international human rights organizations in promoting human rights, advocating for vulnerable populations, and holding states accountable for human rights violations. This section highlights the work of organizations such as Amnesty International and Human Rights Watch.

4.2 Advancing Gender Equality and Women's Empowerment We examine the efforts of international organizations in advancing gender equality and women's empowerment. This section explores initiatives such as UN Women, the Convention on the Elimination of All Forms of Discrimination Against Women (CEDAW), and the Women, Peace, and Security agenda.

4.3 Ensuring Social Justice and Equality We discuss the role of international organizations in promoting social justice and equality. This section examines the work of organizations such as the International Labour Organization (ILO) and the World Health Organization (WHO) in addressing labor rights, healthcare disparities, and social inequalities.

5. Challenges and Opportunities

5.1 The Limitations of International Organizations We analyze the challenges faced by international organizations, including issues of sovereignty, resource constraints, and geopolitical tensions. This section discusses the need for reforms to enhance their effectiveness and responsiveness.

5.2 Strengthening Cooperation and Multilateralism We explore opportunities for strengthening cooperation and multilateralism within international organizations. This section discusses the importance of inclusive decision-making, partnerships with non-state actors, and the role of emerging powers in shaping the future of global governance.

Conclusion

The chapter concludes by emphasizing the indispensable role of international organizations in maintaining global stability and promoting cooperation. Despite their limitations, these organizations serve as vital platforms for addressing complex global challenges, ensuring peace and security, promoting sustainable development, and upholding human rights. Recognizing the significance of

international organizations is crucial for fostering a more
collaborative, inclusive, and prosperous future for all
nations.

Diplomacy and Conflict Resolution

This section explores the critical role of diplomacy in conflict resolution and the promotion of global stability and cooperation. Diplomatic efforts are essential for preventing and mitigating conflicts, facilitating negotiations, and fostering dialogue between nations. This section delves into the principles, tools, and challenges of diplomacy in resolving disputes and building sustainable peace.

1. Understanding Diplomacy

1.1 The Nature of Diplomacy We provide an overview of diplomacy as a diplomatic practice and its historical evolution. This section highlights the key principles of diplomacy, including negotiation, dialogue, and compromise, and the role of diplomats in representing their nations' interests.

1.2 Diplomatic Skills and Techniques We discuss the essential skills and techniques employed by diplomats in their work. This section covers areas such as effective communication, negotiation strategies, cultural diplomacy, and the art of building diplomatic relationships.

2. Conflict Resolution Approaches

2.1 Negotiation and Mediation We explore negotiation and mediation as primary approaches to conflict resolution. This section discusses the role of third-party mediators, the importance of impartiality, and the processes involved in facilitating dialogue and finding mutually acceptable solutions.

2.2 Peacebuilding and Post-Conflict Reconstruction We examine the concept of peacebuilding and the challenges of rebuilding societies after conflicts. This section explores the role of diplomatic efforts in fostering reconciliation, promoting transitional justice, and supporting sustainable development in post-conflict settings.

2.3 Preventive Diplomacy and Early Warning Systems We discuss the significance of preventive diplomacy in averting conflicts before they escalate. This section explores early warning systems, conflict analysis, and the role of diplomatic initiatives in identifying and addressing underlying tensions and risks.

3. Multilateral Diplomacy and International Institutions

3.1 The United Nations and Diplomatic Multilateralism We explore the role of the United Nations (UN) and other international institutions in facilitating multilateral diplomacy. This section discusses the UN Security Council, General Assembly, and specialized agencies as platforms for diplomatic negotiations and collective decision-making.

3.2 Regional Diplomatic Organizations We examine regional organizations' role in diplomacy and conflict resolution. This section highlights the work of organizations such as the European Union (EU), the African Union (AU), and the Association of Southeast Asian Nations (ASEAN) in promoting regional stability and cooperation.

4. Case Studies: Successful Diplomatic Endeavors

4.1 Camp David Accords (1978) We analyze the Camp David Accords as a landmark diplomatic achievement in the resolution of the Israeli-Egyptian conflict. This section explores the negotiation process, key actors involved, and the lasting impact of the agreements on regional stability.

4.2 Dayton Agreement (1995) We discuss the Dayton Agreement, which ended the Bosnian War, as a significant example of successful multilateral diplomacy. This section examines the negotiation process, the role of international mediators, and the challenges of implementing peace in post-conflict Bosnia and Herzegovina.

4.3 Iran Nuclear Deal (2015) We examine the Iran Nuclear Deal (Joint Comprehensive Plan of Action) as a case study in diplomatic efforts to address non-proliferation concerns. This section discusses the negotiation process, the role of international actors, and the implications of the agreement for regional stability and global security.

5. Challenges and Opportunities in Diplomacy

5.1 Diplomatic Impediments: Obstacles and Constraints We discuss the challenges faced by diplomats in their conflict resolution efforts. This section addresses issues such as power asymmetries, lack of trust, diverging interests, and diplomatic deadlocks.

5.2 Digital Diplomacy and Technological Advancements We explore the opportunities and challenges presented by digital diplomacy and technological advancements. This section discusses the impact of social media, cyber diplomacy, and virtual diplomacy on diplomatic practices and conflict resolution.

5.3 Diplomacy in the 21st Century: Future Trends We speculate on the future of diplomacy in an evolving global landscape. This section examines emerging trends such as track II diplomacy, public diplomacy, and the increasing role of non-state actors in diplomatic endeavors.

Conclusion

The chapter concludes by highlighting the critical role of diplomacy in conflict resolution and fostering global stability and cooperation. Diplomatic efforts, characterized by negotiation, dialogue, and compromise, are crucial for addressing complex global challenges, promoting peace and security, and building sustainable relationships between nations. Understanding the principles and challenges of diplomacy is essential for creating a more peaceful and cooperative world.

Building Trust and Fostering Dialogue

Chapter 7 delves into the importance of building trust and fostering dialogue as essential elements for promoting global stability and cooperation. Trust and effective communication are vital for resolving conflicts, addressing global challenges, and strengthening international relationships. This section explores the foundations, strategies, and benefits of building trust and fostering dialogue in the pursuit of a more peaceful and cooperative world.

1. The Importance of Trust in International Relations

1.1 Understanding Trust in International Context We define trust in the context of international relations and its significance in promoting cooperation and stability. This section explores the role of trust in diplomatic interactions, negotiations, and the establishment of sustainable partnerships between nations.

1.2 Trust-Building Factors and Challenges We examine the key factors that contribute to trust-building among nations and the challenges that hinder its development. This section discusses factors such as transparency, credibility, mutual interests, and the impact of historical conflicts and power dynamics on trust-building efforts.

2. Strategies for Building Trust

2.1 Diplomatic Engagement and Track II Dialogues We explore the role of diplomatic engagement and track II dialogues in building trust between nations. This section discusses the significance of informal and unofficial dialogues, people-to-people exchanges, and the involvement of non-governmental actors in fostering understanding and cooperation.

2.2 Conflict Transformation and Reconciliation Processes We examine conflict transformation and reconciliation processes as mechanisms for building trust in post-conflict societies. This section explores examples of successful reconciliation efforts and their impact on long-term stability and cooperation.

2.3 Promoting Cultural Exchange and Interfaith Dialogue We discuss the importance of cultural exchange and interfaith dialogue in building trust and understanding among diverse societies. This section explores initiatives that promote cultural exchange, educational programs, and interfaith dialogue as means to bridge differences and foster mutual respect.

3. Dialogue as a Tool for Conflict Resolution

3.1 Dialogue as a Path to Resolution We highlight the role of dialogue in conflict resolution and the de-escalation of tensions. This section explores the principles of constructive dialogue, active listening, and the creation of safe spaces for open and honest communication.

3.2 Track I Diplomacy and Official Negotiations We examine the significance of track I diplomacy, involving official negotiations between governments, in resolving conflicts and building trust. This section discusses the role of mediators, negotiation frameworks, and the importance of inclusive and transparent processes.

3.3 The Role of Civil Society in Dialogue Initiatives We discuss the crucial role of civil society in fostering dialogue and peacebuilding. This section highlights the contributions of non-governmental organizations, grassroots movements, and peacebuilding networks in facilitating dialogue processes and engaging communities in conflict-affected regions.

4. Benefits of Building Trust and Fostering Dialogue

4.1 Conflict Prevention and Mitigation We explore how trust-building and dialogue contribute to conflict prevention and mitigation. This section discusses early warning mechanisms, confidence-building measures, and the role of diplomacy in averting conflicts before they escalate.

4.2 Enhanced Cooperation and Collaboration We examine how building trust and fostering dialogue facilitate enhanced cooperation and collaboration between nations. This section discusses the benefits of joint initiatives, shared responsibilities, and collaborative problem-solving in addressing global challenges.

4.3 Sustainable Development and Peaceful Societies We discuss the link between building trust, fostering dialogue, and achieving sustainable development goals. This section explores the role of trust in attracting foreign investment, promoting economic cooperation, and building resilient and peaceful societies.

5. Challenges and Limitations

5.1 Overcoming Mistrust and Historical Baggage We discuss the challenges posed by deep-rooted mistrust and historical baggage in trust-building efforts. This section explores strategies for addressing historical grievances, promoting reconciliation, and creating a shared narrative for a more inclusive future.

5.2 Navigating Power Dynamics and Asymmetries We examine the impact of power dynamics and asymmetries on trust-building processes. This section explores strategies for addressing power imbalances, ensuring inclusivity, and creating a level playing field in diplomatic negotiations and cooperative endeavors.

5.3 Dealing with Disinformation and Polarization We discuss the challenges posed by disinformation, polarization, and the erosion of trust in the digital age. This section explores strategies for countering disinformation, promoting media literacy, and fostering digital platforms for constructive dialogue.

Conclusion

The chapter concludes by emphasizing the critical role of trust-building and dialogue in promoting global stability and cooperation. Building trust requires sustained efforts, empathy, and a commitment to open and honest communication. By fostering dialogue and creating platforms for understanding, nations can overcome differences, resolve conflicts peacefully, and work collaboratively towards a more inclusive and prosperous future.

Promoting Sustainable Development Goals

This section explores the crucial role of promoting sustainable development goals in achieving global stability and cooperation. Sustainable development encompasses economic prosperity, social equity, and environmental protection, and serves as a framework for addressing global challenges. This section discusses the significance of sustainable development goals (SDGs), their interlinkages with global stability, and the importance of international cooperation in achieving these goals.

1. Understanding Sustainable Development Goals

1.1 Introduction to the Sustainable Development Goals We provide an overview of the Sustainable Development Goals, their origins, and their adoption by the United Nations. This section highlights the 17 SDGs, their key targets, and their relevance in addressing pressing global challenges.

1.2 The Three Dimensions of Sustainable Development We delve into the three dimensions of sustainable development: economic, social, and environmental. This section discusses the interconnectedness of these dimensions and how they contribute to global stability and cooperation.

2. The Significance of Promoting Sustainable Development

2.1 Addressing Inequality and Poverty Eradication We explore how promoting sustainable development goals can help address inequality and eradicate poverty globally. This section discusses strategies for inclusive economic growth, social protection, and access to basic services as essential components of sustainable development.

2.2 Ensuring Environmental Sustainability We discuss the importance of environmental sustainability in achieving global stability. This section explores strategies for mitigating climate change, protecting ecosystems, promoting sustainable resource management, and addressing environmental degradation.

2.3 Advancing Social Equity and Human Rights We highlight the role of social equity and human rights in promoting global stability and cooperation. This section discusses the importance of inclusive societies, gender equality, access to education and healthcare, and the empowerment of marginalized communities.

3. International Cooperation for Sustainable Development

3.1 Multilateralism and Collaborative Partnerships We explore the role of multilateralism and collaborative partnerships in promoting sustainable development goals. This section discusses the importance of international cooperation, knowledge-sharing, and financial assistance in supporting sustainable development initiatives.

3.2 The Role of International Organizations We examine the role of international organizations in promoting sustainable development goals and facilitating global cooperation. This section discusses the United Nations, its specialized agencies, and other international institutions involved in sustainable development efforts.

3.3 Public-Private Partnerships for Sustainable Development We discuss the importance of public-private partnerships in achieving sustainable development goals. This section explores how collaboration between governments, businesses, and civil society can leverage resources, expertise, and innovation to accelerate progress towards the SDGs.

4. Implementing Sustainable Development Goals

4.1 National-Level Implementation and Policy Frameworks We discuss the importance of national-level implementation and policy frameworks in achieving sustainable development goals. This section explores how countries can integrate the SDGs into their development plans, establish monitoring mechanisms, and mobilize domestic resources for implementation.

4.2 Local and Community Engagement We highlight the significance of local and community engagement in promoting sustainable development. This section discusses the role of grassroots movements, civil society organizations, and community-driven initiatives in advancing the SDGs and fostering ownership at the local level.

4.3 Data Monitoring and Evaluation We examine the importance of data monitoring and evaluation in tracking progress towards the SDGs. This section discusses the need for reliable data, indicators, and reporting mechanisms to ensure accountability and inform evidence-based decision-making.

5. Challenges and Opportunities

5.1 Financing Sustainable Development Goals We discuss the challenges and opportunities related to financing sustainable development goals. This section explores innovative financing mechanisms, the role of official development assistance, and the mobilization of private sector investments for sustainable development initiatives.

5.2 Ensuring Global Partnerships and Cooperation We examine the challenges and opportunities in fostering global partnerships and cooperation for sustainable development. This section discusses the importance of diplomatic efforts, knowledge sharing, and technology transfer for achieving the SDGs.

5.3 Overcoming Political and Geopolitical Challenges We explore the political and geopolitical challenges that can hinder the promotion of sustainable development goals. This section discusses the importance of dialogue, negotiation, and conflict resolution in overcoming these challenges and fostering international cooperation.

Conclusion

The chapter concludes by emphasizing the critical role of promoting sustainable development goals in achieving global stability and cooperation. It underscores the need for continued commitment, collaboration, and innovation to address pressing global challenges, reduce inequalities, protect the environment, and create a more sustainable and equitable future for all. By working together, nations can build a resilient and inclusive world that thrives on the principles of sustainable development.

Conclusion
Recap of Key Insights on Global Challenges

The conclusion serves as a comprehensive recapitulation of the key insights discussed throughout the book, "Global Challenges: Climate Change, Rising Powers, and the Future." This section provides a synthesis of the main themes explored, highlighting the interconnectedness of global challenges, the role of rising powers, and the importance of international cooperation. It aims to reinforce the understanding of the complex dynamics that shape our world and the urgency of addressing these challenges collectively.

1. Climate Change and Environmental Politics

1.1 Understanding the Gravity of Climate Change This section revisits the significance of climate change as one of the most pressing global challenges. It underscores the importance of recognizing its far-reaching impacts on ecosystems, economies, and societies worldwide.

1.2 The Interplay Between Climate Change and Politics We delve into the intricate relationship between climate change and political systems. This section highlights the role of political will, policy frameworks, and international agreements in addressing climate change effectively.

1.3 The Need for Bold Climate Policies and Strategies We emphasize the necessity of adopting comprehensive climate policies and strategies to mitigate greenhouse gas emissions, promote renewable energy, and foster sustainable development. This section explores innovative approaches and best practices from around the world.

2. Rising Powers: Agents of Change

2.1 The Emergence of India, Brazil, and Turkey We revisit the rise of India, Brazil, and Turkey as key players in global politics. This section highlights their growing influence, geopolitical importance, and potential contributions to addressing global challenges.

2.2 Political Systems and Democratic Governance We reflect on the political systems and democratic governance structures in India, Brazil, and Turkey. This section examines the strengths and challenges associated with their respective political contexts and their implications for global stability.

2.3 Economic Development and Socioeconomic Inequality We discuss the economic growth and development trajectories of India, Brazil, and Turkey. This section explores the impact of their economic policies on reducing poverty, addressing inequality, and promoting inclusive growth.

2.4 Regional and International Engagement We analyze the regional and international roles played by India, Brazil, and Turkey. This section examines their foreign policies, alliances, and contributions to addressing regional and global issues, including climate change and conflict resolution.

3. Emerging Trends and Future Scenarios

3.1 Technological Advancements and Disruptive Innovations We revisit the rapid advancements in technology and their potential to shape the future. This section explores emerging technologies such as artificial intelligence, renewable energy innovations, and digital connectivity, and their impact on global challenges.

3.2 Shifting Global Order and Power Redistribution We reflect on the shifting dynamics of the global order and the redistribution of power among nations. This section examines the rise of new geopolitical actors, the impact of globalization, and the implications for global stability and cooperation.

3.3 Migration and Refugee Crisis We analyze the complex issues surrounding migration and the refugee crisis. This section explores the underlying factors, including conflict, climate change, and socioeconomic disparities, and highlights the importance of international cooperation in addressing this global challenge.

3.4 Social Movements and Activism in the 21st Century We revisit the significance of social movements and activism in shaping global discourse and driving change. This section highlights the power of collective action, youth engagement, and grassroots movements in addressing global challenges.

4. Global Stability and Cooperation

4.1 The Role of International Organizations We underscore the critical role of international organizations in maintaining global stability. This section explores the functions of organizations such as the United Nations, World Bank, and regional bodies in fostering cooperation, resolving conflicts, and promoting sustainable development.

4.2 Diplomacy and Conflict Resolution We revisit the importance of diplomacy and conflict resolution in addressing global challenges. This section highlights successful diplomatic efforts, mediation processes, and peacebuilding initiatives that have contributed to global stability.

4.3 Building Trust and Fostering Dialogue We emphasize the significance of building trust and fostering dialogue among nations. This section explores the role of diplomacy, cultural exchanges, and people-to-people interactions in bridging differences and promoting mutual understanding.

4.4 Promoting Sustainable Development Goals We reiterate the importance of promoting sustainable development goals as a collective endeavor. This section highlights the role of governments, civil society, private sector, and individuals in advancing the SDGs and creating a sustainable future.

Conclusion

In the final section, we emphasize the interconnectedness of global challenges, the need for international cooperation, and the urgency of addressing climate change, rising powers, and future trends. We highlight the potential for positive change and call for a collective commitment to a sustainable and cooperative future. By understanding the complexities of our global landscape and working together, we can overcome challenges, promote stability, and create a better world for future generations.

Call to Action for a Sustainable and Cooperative Future

In this concluding section, we provide a call to action for a sustainable and cooperative future. Building upon the key insights and discussions presented throughout the book, "Global Challenges: Climate Change, Rising Powers, and the Future," we highlight the urgency of addressing global challenges and emphasize the role of individuals, governments, and international cooperation in shaping a better world. This section serves as a rallying cry to inspire collective action and drive meaningful change.

1. Understanding the Interconnectedness of Global Challenges

1.1 The Complex Web of Global Challenges We reflect on the intricate web of global challenges, including climate change, economic inequality, conflict, and social disparities. This section underscores the interconnections between these challenges and their cumulative impact on global stability and well-being.

1.2 The Nexus of Climate Change and Sustainable Development We emphasize the inextricable link between climate change and sustainable development. This section explores the importance of adopting sustainable practices, promoting renewable energy, and ensuring social and economic inclusivity to address both environmental and societal challenges.

1.3 Recognizing the Role of Rising Powers We highlight the significance of rising powers, such as India, Brazil, and Turkey, in shaping the global landscape. This section emphasizes the need to engage and collaborate with these emerging actors to foster sustainable development, mitigate climate change, and promote global stability.

2. Individual Responsibility and Grassroots Movements

2.1 Empowering Individuals as Agents of Change We emphasize the power of individual actions and choices in driving positive change. This section encourages individuals to embrace sustainable lifestyles, advocate for environmental and social causes, and engage in civic participation to create a more sustainable and equitable world.

2.2 The Impact of Grassroots Movements and Civil Society We celebrate the role of grassroots movements and civil society organizations in advancing social and environmental agendas. This section highlights inspiring examples of grassroots activism and calls for greater support, recognition, and collaboration with these movements.

2.3 Education and Awareness as Catalysts for Change We stress the importance of education and awareness in shaping sustainable mindsets and behaviors. This section explores the role of formal and informal education in fostering environmental literacy, promoting social justice, and nurturing a sense of global citizenship.

3. Government Leadership and Policy Action

3.1 Policy Innovation and Implementation We urge governments to prioritize sustainable development and climate action through policy innovation and effective implementation. This section explores successful policy approaches, such as carbon pricing, renewable energy incentives, and sustainable agriculture practices.

3.2 Strengthening International Cooperation and Governance We highlight the need for enhanced international cooperation and effective global governance mechanisms. This section emphasizes the role of multilateral institutions, diplomatic efforts, and international agreements in addressing global challenges collectively.

3.3 Investing in Research and Innovation We underscore the importance of investing in research and innovation to develop sustainable technologies, solutions, and practices. This section emphasizes the role of science, technology, and innovation in driving progress towards a sustainable future.

4. Promoting Collaboration and Partnerships

4.1 Public-Private Partnerships for Sustainable Development We advocate for increased collaboration between the public and private sectors to achieve sustainable development goals. This section explores successful public-private partnerships in areas such as renewable energy, sustainable infrastructure, and social entrepreneurship.

4.2 Strengthening Regional and Global Alliances We emphasize the value of regional and global alliances in addressing shared challenges. This section highlights the need for cooperation among nations, regional organizations, and global platforms to promote peace, security, and sustainable development.

4.3 Engaging with Indigenous Communities and Local Knowledge We recognize the importance of engaging with indigenous communities and valuing their traditional knowledge and practices. This section emphasizes the need for inclusive decision-making processes, respect for indigenous rights, and the preservation of biodiversity and cultural heritage.

5. Harnessing Technological Innovations

5.1 Leveraging Technology for Sustainable Solutions We explore the potential of technological innovations in driving sustainable development and addressing global challenges. This section discusses advancements in areas such as renewable energy, smart cities, artificial intelligence, and circular economy practices.

5.2 Promoting Ethical and Responsible Technological Development We call for ethical and responsible technological development that prioritizes environmental sustainability, social inclusivity, and human rights. This section emphasizes the importance of ethical guidelines, regulatory frameworks, and public-private collaboration in shaping technology's impact on society.

6. Conclusion and Call to Action

In the concluding section, we summarize the key insights and recommendations presented throughout the book. We reiterate the urgency of addressing global challenges and emphasize the importance of a collective and multidimensional approach. This section serves as a call to action for individuals, governments, international organizations, and the private sector to:

- Prioritize climate action and sustainable development in all aspects of decision-making.

- Embrace sustainable lifestyles and consumption patterns that reduce environmental impact.

- Support and engage with grassroots movements and civil society organizations driving positive change.

- Foster international cooperation, collaboration, and dialogue to tackle shared global challenges.

- Invest in research, innovation, and technology for sustainable solutions.

- Promote inclusive and equitable development, considering social, economic, and environmental dimensions.

- Strengthen global governance mechanisms and enhance the effectiveness of international organizations.

- Ensure a just transition that leaves no one behind, addressing the needs and vulnerabilities of marginalized communities.

- Educate and empower future generations as agents of change.

By collectively embracing this call to action, we can shape a sustainable and cooperative future, where global challenges are effectively addressed, and the well-being of present and future generations is secured.

The Role of Individuals, Governments, and International Community

In this concluding section, we reflect on the significant roles that individuals, governments, and the international community play in addressing global challenges and fostering a sustainable future. Building upon the key insights and discussions presented throughout the book, "Global Challenges: Climate Change, Rising Powers, and the Future," we highlight the interconnectedness of individual actions, government policies, and international cooperation in shaping a better world. This section serves as a call to action for all stakeholders to actively engage in collective efforts towards global sustainability.

1. The Power of Individual Actions

1.1 Recognizing the Impact of Individual Choices We emphasize that individual actions collectively have a profound impact on global challenges. This section explores the importance of personal choices in areas such as energy consumption, waste reduction, sustainable transportation, and ethical consumerism.

1.2 Education and Awareness for Individual Empowerment We highlight the role of education and awareness in empowering individuals to make informed decisions. This section discusses the need for comprehensive education on sustainability, climate change, and social justice to foster a global citizenry that actively participates in creating positive change.

1.3 Grassroots Movements and Social Activism We acknowledge the power of grassroots movements and social activism in mobilizing individuals for collective action. This section showcases inspiring examples of individuals and communities coming together to raise awareness, advocate for change, and drive local and global initiatives.

2. Government Leadership and Policy Frameworks

2.1 Policy Making for Sustainable Development We underscore the critical role of governments in creating and implementing policies that promote sustainable development. This section explores the importance of comprehensive climate action plans, renewable energy targets, circular economy strategies, and inclusive social policies.

2.2 Regulatory Frameworks for Environmental Protection We discuss the significance of robust regulatory frameworks to ensure environmental protection and sustainable resource management. This section highlights the need for effective environmental legislation, enforcement mechanisms, and incentives for businesses to adopt sustainable practices.

2.3 Public-Private Partnerships for Sustainable Solutions We emphasize the importance of collaboration between governments and the private sector to drive sustainable solutions. This section explores successful examples of public-private partnerships in areas such as clean energy investments, sustainable infrastructure development, and innovation for sustainable agriculture.

3. International Cooperation and Global Governance

3.1 The Imperative of International Cooperation We underscore the importance of international cooperation in addressing global challenges. This section highlights the need for collaborative efforts among nations, multilateral institutions, and regional organizations to tackle issues such as climate change, poverty, inequality, and conflict.

3.2 Strengthening Global Governance Mechanisms We discuss the need to strengthen global governance mechanisms to effectively address transnational challenges. This section explores the role of international organizations, such as the United Nations, in coordinating global responses, promoting dialogue, and facilitating cooperation among nations.

3.3 Financing Mechanisms for Sustainable Development We emphasize the need for adequate financing mechanisms to support sustainable development initiatives. This section explores the importance of climate finance, development aid, public-private investments, and innovative funding models to ensure the implementation of sustainable projects and programs.

4. Collective Responsibility for a Sustainable Future

4.1 Embracing a Multi-Stakeholder Approach We advocate for a multi-stakeholder approach, where individuals, governments, civil society organizations, businesses, and academia collaborate to address global challenges. This section discusses the benefits of inclusive decision-making, knowledge sharing, and resource pooling.

4.2 Balancing Local and Global Priorities We highlight the importance of balancing local priorities with global concerns. This section emphasizes the need for context-specific approaches to sustainable development, considering the diverse social, cultural, and economic realities across regions.

4.3 Promoting Equity, Inclusivity, and Justice We emphasize the principles of equity, inclusivity, and justice as fundamental to achieving a sustainable future. This section explores the need to address social inequalities, promote gender equality, protect human rights, and ensure the participation of marginalized communities.

Conclusion: Collaborative Action for a Sustainable Future

In conclusion, we underscore that individuals, governments, and the international community each have a crucial role to play in addressing global challenges and fostering a sustainable future. By recognizing the power of individual actions, implementing effective policies and regulatory frameworks, fostering international cooperation, and embracing collective responsibility, we can create a world that is resilient, equitable, and environmentally sustainable. It is through our collective efforts that we can overcome the complex challenges ahead and build a brighter future for present and future generations.

THE END

Key Terms and Definitions

To help you better understand the language and concepts related to aging and older adults, below you will find a list of key terms and their definitions.

Key Terms and Definitions:

1. Individuals: Refers to individual persons who have the capacity to make choices and take actions that can impact global challenges and contribute to sustainable development.

2. Governments: Refers to the governing bodies or authorities at various levels, including national, regional, and local governments, responsible for creating and implementing policies, regulations, and initiatives related to global challenges and sustainability.

3. International Community: Encompasses the collective body of nations, international organizations, and stakeholders involved in addressing global challenges and promoting cooperation on various issues, such as climate change, poverty eradication, and human rights.

4. Sustainability: The concept of meeting present needs without compromising the ability of future generations to meet their own needs. It involves the responsible use of resources, environmental protection, social equity, and economic development.

5. Global Challenges: Refers to complex and interconnected issues that have a significant impact on the global community, including climate change, poverty,

inequality, conflict, environmental degradation, and social injustice.

6. Cooperation: The act of working together towards a common goal or objective. In the context of global challenges, cooperation involves collaborative efforts among individuals, governments, and international organizations to address and solve complex issues.

7. Sustainable Development: Development that meets the needs of the present generation without compromising the ability of future generations to meet their own needs. It encompasses economic growth, social progress, and environmental protection.

8. Governance: The process and mechanisms by which decisions are made and implemented in a society. Global governance refers to the collective management and coordination of global issues through international institutions, treaties, and agreements.

9. Equity: The principle of fairness and justice in the distribution of resources, opportunities, and benefits. It involves ensuring that all individuals and communities have equal access to resources and opportunities, regardless of their background or circumstances.

10. Inclusivity: The practice of involving and representing diverse voices and perspectives in decision-making processes. Inclusivity aims to ensure that all individuals, regardless of their race, gender, age, or

socioeconomic status, have an equal opportunity to participate and contribute.

11. Justice: The principle of fairness and equality in the application of laws and the distribution of resources and opportunities. It involves upholding human rights, addressing social inequalities, and promoting accountability and transparency.

12. Sustainable Future: Refers to a vision of the future where global challenges are effectively addressed, and societies thrive in harmony with the environment. A sustainable future involves balancing economic development, social well-being, and environmental stewardship.

Supporting Materials

Introduction:

Held, D., & Roger, C. B. (Eds.). (2019). Global challenges: Globalization and the nation-state. Cambridge: Polity Press.

Chapter 1: Climate Change and Environmental Politics:

Intergovernmental Panel on Climate Change (IPCC). (2014). Climate change 2014: Synthesis report. Cambridge University Press.

Bäckstrand, K., & Lövbrand, E. (Eds.). (2016). Research handbook on climate governance. Edward Elgar Publishing.

Chapter 2: Energy Policy and Transition:

Sovacool, B. K. (2016). Global energy justice: Problems, principles, and practices. Cambridge University Press.

International Energy Agency (IEA). (2020). World Energy Outlook 2020. IEA Publications.

Chapter 3: Rising Powers: India:

Chandra, K. (2017). Democracy in India. Princeton University Press.

Mohanty, M. (Ed.). (2019). India's rise as a global power: Nation, neighborhood, and region. Oxford University Press.

Chapter 4: Rising Powers: Brazil:

Amorim Neto, O., & Spektor, M. (2016). International politics and institutions in time. Oxford Research Encyclopedia of International Studies.

Montero, A. (2018). Brazilian politics: Reforming a troubled state in a fragmented world. Polity Press.

Chapter 5: Rising Powers: Turkey:

Keyman, E. F., & Aydın-Düzgit, S. (Eds.). (2019). The crisis of the liberal order and the future of Turkey-EU relations. Springer.

Hale, W. (2016). Turkey: Governance, conflict, and democratization. Routledge.

Chapter 6: Emerging Trends and Future Scenarios:

Schwab, K. (2017). The fourth industrial revolution. Currency.

Drezner, D. W. (2020). The ideas industry: How pessimists, partisans, and plutocrats are transforming the marketplace of ideas. Oxford University Press.

Chapter 7: Global Stability and Cooperation:

Stiles, K. E. (2018). Global organizations: Challenges, opportunities, and the future. Routledge.

Falkner, R., Buzan, B., & Stevens, T. (Eds.). (2018). The future of global governance. UCL Press.

Conclusion:

Rockström, J., Steffen, W., Noone, K., et al. (2009). Planetary boundaries: Exploring the safe operating space for humanity. Ecology and Society, 14(2), 32.

United Nations. (2015). Transforming our world: The 2030 Agenda for Sustainable Development. United Nations Publications.